GARDENING BY DESIGN

WARD·LOCK

CONTAINER GARDENING

ALAN TOOGOOD

GARDENING BY DESIGN

WARD · LOCK

CONTAINER GARDENING

ALAN TOOGOOD

WARD LOCK

ACKNOWLEDGEMENTS

All the colour photographs were taken by Bob Challinor.

The publishers are grateful to the following garden owners for granting permission for their gardens to be photographed: The Director, Hever Castle, Edenbridge, Kent (pp. 10, 11, 15); The Lord Northbourne (pp. 14, 18, 23); Mr & Mrs V. Whittingham, (pp. 19, 58); The Royal Horticultural Society (pp. 22, 54, 55, 59); The Royal Horticultural Society/*House & Garden* magazine (p.67); Lys de Bray (pp. 30, 62); Arthur Billitt (p. 31); Idencroft Herb Nursery (pp. 46, 66); Bob Challinor (p. 47); and Major and Mrs P. D. Birchall (p. 51).

All the line drawings are by Nils Solberg. Fig. 11 is after an illustration from the Bradstone catalogue.

Text & illustrations © Ward Lock Ltd 1988

This edition first published in Great Britain
in 1990 by Ward Lock Limited, Villiers House,
41-47 Strand, London, WC2N 5JE, a Cassell company

Reprinted 1990, 1991

House editor Denis Ingram

Text set in Bembo Roman
by TJB Photosetting Limited, South Witham, Lincolnshire

Printed and bound in Spain by Graficas Reunidas

British Library Cataloguing in Publication Data

Toogood, Alan R.
    Container gardening.—(Gardening by
design)
    1. Container gardening
    I. Title   II. Series
    635′.048   SB418

ISBN 0-7063-6896-7

CONTENTS

PREFACE 6

1   ANCIENT AND MODERN 8

2   GARDEN ORNAMENTS 12

3   AROUND THE HOUSE 21

4   COLOUR ON THE PATIO 33

5   MINI-GARDENS 49

6   DESIGN IDEAS FOR UTILITY PLANTS 64

7   PREPARATIONS AND CARE 71

INDEX 77

APPENDIX 80

PREFACE

Pots, urns and other containers have been used for growing plants since ancient times and today they play a major role in garden design. The garden centres are packed with them, and there are several specialist suppliers who offer both antique containers and replicas of traditional designs.

There can scarcely be a garden without some kind of container, whether a tub or urn on a patio, a hanging basket or window box, a growing-bag for tomatoes, or a raised bed or sink planted with alpines.

Containers must, however, be chosen with care, for they should suit the style of the house and garden. For instance, a modern concrete bowl would look fine in a formal, contemporary town garden, but completely out of place in a country or cottage garden. Wooden and traditional terracotta or stone containers would be far more suitable for the latter.

Containers do not have to be planted; highly ornamental kinds, like richly decorated Florentine urns, are ornaments in their own right and make marvellous focal points in a garden. However, most people will want to plant the majority of their containers and again great care should be taken in choosing suitable plants for them, making sure they are in harmony with both the containers and the style of the house and garden.

All too often people choose temporary plants for containers, such as spring and summer bedding plants. There is nothing wrong with this, although seasonal bedding can be rather labour-intensive. You can certainly vary the displays from year to year and co-ordinate colours with the house. But on the other hand there is a wealth of permanent plants which thrive in containers, like shrubs, climbers and hardy perennials, and I would highly recommend devoting some of your containers to them, especially to provide a permanent 'framework', around which you can vary the mood and colour scheme with temporary plants.

A collection of planted containers should be capable of providing colour and interest all the year round, and this is particularly important in very small gardens where containers often form the major means of growing plants.

Many fruits and vegetables make ideal subjects for containers on the patio but these utility plants need not look out of place in the overall design of the garden as they can be made to harmonize with ornamental plants. Indeed, dwarf fruit trees grown in traditional square wooden tubs can make most attractive features on the patio.

Ideally containers should be taken into account when designing a garden – they should appear to be part of the overall design and not simply added haphazardly as an afterthought. They should have some definite purpose, a particular role to play, whether as ornaments to act as focal points or create atmosphere, or to help provide colour and interest in some particular part of the garden – perhaps immediately around the house or on a patio.

Every gardener, whether the owner of a very tiny or large garden, or whose aim is to provide colour on a balcony, can make use of containers. I hope that this book, which is rounded off with general practical advice on growing in containers, will inspire you with some fresh ideas.

A. T.

A classical-style terracotta urn acts as a focal point in this garden, drawing the eye to a bed of antirrhinums. Not all containers have to be planted.

1

ANCIENT AND MODERN

For thousands of years plants have been grown in containers by many civilizations. The ancient Egyptians, Greeks and Chinese had earthenware pots, and the Chinese also produced handsome ceramic pots. The Romans had a wide variety, both as ornaments and for growing plants. They included them on their roof gardens and even had window boxes.

All kinds of pots, and window boxes, were used in Medieval Europe and they were made of various materials like clay or terracotta, metal and even wattle (woven strips of wood).

Throughout history terracotta clay has been the most widely used material for pots and other containers, no doubt because it has always been readily available and easily worked, even into quite intricate designs. Stone, lead and wood were also widely used. Round or square wooden tubs were once commonly used for growing citrus and other fruits.

We can buy containers today in all of these materials (except wattle). Mass-produced terracotta flower pots date from the early nineteenth century and indeed the Victorians often used them, together with terracotta window boxes. The Victorians had all styles of containers, including very ornate designs of their own. They mass-produced metal window boxes too.

In past centuries some of the most beautiful and highly ornate earthenware urns and pots were produced in Italy, especially in Florence and Venice. Copies of these are very popular today, adding style and elegance to gardens and patios.

Today there is a vast range of ornamental containers to choose from. There are reproductions of many of the classical styles – Greek, Roman, Chinese, Italian, Victorian and so on – and very popular they are too. There are also many modern, twentieth-century styles that are particularly useful for associating with contemporary architecture. For instance, the shallow concrete bowl, which first appeared at the Festival of Britain.

I have already mentioned that most of the traditional materials are still used for making containers today, but there are also containers in various modern materials, like concrete, reconstituted stone, fibreglass and plastics. Terracotta is still widely used and although clay pots are often imported from Italy and Spain, there are some British manufacturers (a trend is towards frost-proof terracotta pots). The U.S.A. imports clay pots from Mexico.

WHY USE CONTAINERS?

Obviously containers have to be used for growing plants if you do not have a garden – for instance, if all your gardening is done on a balcony or perhaps in a basement. But why use containers if you have a garden? There are several very good reasons, mainly to do with garden design.

Firstly, containers can be used as ornaments in their own right, perhaps to create a particular mood or atmosphere in the garden. For example, on a patio one can create a Mediterranean atmosphere by choosing the right styles of containers. Or if you are designing an Oriental garden then the use of Chinese glazed terracotta pots would certainly create the right atmosphere. Likewise a formal Italian-style garden could be embellished with Florentine urns and pots.

A 'rustic' atmosphere can be created in an English cottage or country garden by using wooden tubs and barrels as ornaments. Lead urns and cisterns, as well as stone containers, would also create the right mood.

Containers can be used as focal points to draw the eye to various parts of a garden. For instance, they can be set at the end of a vista or at the bend in a path. They can be used for framing steps and the doors of the house. In other words, ornamental containers can be used just like vases and other ornaments in interior decoration.

Containers, though, are mainly used for displaying plants and therefore are more often than not planted. Even if you have a garden, planted containers are still very useful for they allow you to easily place colour where it is needed. Again the obvious place is on a patio, but you can also introduce colour to other areas, such as porches, driveways, paths, sitting areas, etc.

Hanging baskets and window boxes allow you to bring colour and interest to the house itself, in the same way as wall pots which are fixed direct to the house walls. Hanging baskets can also provide much-needed colour on pergolas, garages and sheds.

Containers can be an integral part of the garden layout, in the form of raised beds and borders, double walls filled with soil for planting, and very large planters. These can all legitimately be classed as containers, for they hold soil in which plants are grown. Generally, raised beds and borders are used to create a variation in height on a flat plot, while double walls are often used as front boundaries, to front a porch and for surrounding patios. Very large permanent planters are often featured on patios; they allow more imaginative planting schemes than conventional containers.

Rock gardens are expensive to build and space-consuming but many people have discovered that an attractive alternative method of growing alpines is to create miniature rock gardens in sinks – either genuine old stone sinks or converted glazed ones.

Often in small gardens the only way to grow fruits and vegetables is in containers on a patio. Fruit trees are, of course, very ornamental in their own right but can be further enhanced by choosing distinctive containers for them.

The growing-bag (a compost-filled plastic bag) enables many people to grow vegetables who otherwise would not be able to do so. They can be used on balconies, on patios and in tiny basement gardens for salad crops, many other small vegetables and, of course, for tomatoes. Of all the many types of container available, the purely utilitarian growing-bags are the most unattractive, but this should not deter you from using them, for they can be disguised so that they harmonize with the surroundings.

The introduction some years ago of the proprietary Tower Pot has enabled many people with only limited space to grow strawberries, for the plants are grown vertically. These containers certainly do not look out of place on the modern patio. Cottage owners can, alternatively, grow lots of strawberries in a small area by planting them in strawberry barrels.

Many people do not realize that there is an enormous range of plants that can be grown in containers – all too often we see nothing but spring and summer bedding plants. Certainly these give lots of colour and should by no means be dismissed, but bear in mind that containers of suitable size allow you to grow small trees, shrubs, climbers, roses, conifers, hardy perennials and other plants in very confined spaces – on patios, in the tiny pocket handkerchief garden, in basements and so on.

Containers also allow you to display various tender plants in the summer, to give a sub-tropical atmosphere, say on the patio; the plants being returned indoors or into the greenhouse before the frosts arrive.

Terracotta clay has for centuries been used to make urns and other kinds of container. Classical styles in this material are freely available today.

This large stone container makes a striking focal point in this garden and has been planted with the popular summer bedding plants heliotrope and fibrous-rooted begonias.

11

2

GARDEN ORNAMENTS

Distinctive and perhaps highly decorated containers can be used as garden ornaments in their own right, without necessarily having to be planted. This idea is often used in large gardens, especially when extensive garden maintenance precludes one from having many planted containers.

When using containers as ornaments one should think in terms of quality: it is not a good idea to use cheap containers, such as plastic imitations of classical designs, as these never appear aesthetically pleasing when standing alone, unplanted. On the other hand they are fine where the container is to be densely planted, for example with trailing bedding plants, which will hide most of the container, and where several are to be grouped closely together on a patio.

In general, however, one should think in terms of the better quality containers. In my opinion it is well worth saving specially for a suitable item. Of course, if finances allow, one could not do better than invest in one or two antique containers. I think invest is the right word, for such containers certainly increase in value over the years – they are, after all, collector's items.

Classical urns, vases and pots are very popular for use as isolated garden ornaments, whether originals or imitations. The more ornate the better, for remember they are for decoration and are meant to be admired and enjoyed for their own sake.

Likely sources of suitable containers include garden centres for imitation classical designs, and antique dealers for originals. There are also several specialist suppliers for both reproduction and antique classical containers, and these would be well worth visiting if they are within easy reach.

CONTAINERS AS FOCAL POINTS

A focal point is an object which draws the eye so that one is tempted to walk towards it and admire it more closely. On reaching the focal point you should, in a well-designed garden, suddenly come across another part of the garden, hitherto hidden from view. Focal points direct attention to various parts of the garden and they provide a sense of unity, linking various parts or areas of the garden. Focal points can create a feeling of distance, too, for usually they are positioned at the ends of vistas or long views: for example at the end of a lawn, at the end of a path or in a far corner of the garden. Focal points can also be positioned wherever a path changes direction, to encourage an exploration of the garden.

Many objects may be used as focal points, including statuary and distinctive plants. Ornamental containers are also ideal for the purpose and indeed are often used, especially in large gardens, but in small ones too.

Among the advantages of using containers as focal points can be included the fact that generally they are relatively easy to move around so that you can, if necessary, position a container in several different places until you are completely satisfied that you have found exactly the right site for it.

Containers which are to be used as focal points must be chosen with great care. Not only should they be distinctive but, most important of all, they should suit the size of the garden. In a large garden you will of course need large containers, perhaps urns, vases and bowls

Fig. 1 A classical stone urn on a pedestal makes an impressive focal-point in a large garden but needs a suitable background such as a group of dark green conifers.

gardens where this has been done, but in my opinion it is rather an eccentric approach.

In a modern town garden there is scope for using modern-looking containers as focal points (Fig.2).

Concrete tubs, square or circular, could be clustered together, either of different heights or on different levels to create a kind of sculpture. Also in a modern

Fig. 2 In a town garden modern-looking simulated-stone containers could be clustered together to create a kind of sculpture. Use such an arrangement as a focal point to draw the eye and ensure it has a suitable background, such as the evergreen shrub *Fatsia japonica*.

on pedestals to give height (Fig. 1). In a tiny garden more diminutive containers should be used as focal points.

The style must also be chosen with care, for it must suit the style of the garden. It is a bit outrageous, for instance, to have a very modern-looking container in an informal, period or country garden. I do know of

Warm orangy terracotta containers can make delightful focal points in country gardens. This one is planted with zonal and ivy-leaved pelargoniums for summer colour.

A large garden calls for a really large container to act as a focal point. This bulky stone tub in a traditional style has been permanently planted with an ornamental shrub.

15

garden very plain light-coloured (simulated stone) containers are recommended too, such as urns (those shaped like Ali-baba pots) and vases.

Of course light-coloured containers need a dark background to show them off. In a town garden this might be a fence stained dark brown or it may be a very dark-coloured brick wall – deep red or even grey or blackish. If no suitable background exists, you should consider using a suitable plant as a background: something with dark-coloured foliage. Among the finest shrubs for this purpose are the purple-leaved varieties of the smoke bush, *Cotinus coggygria*, such as 'Royal Purple' with dark wine-purple leaves, or the rich plum purple 'Foliis Purpureis'. *Fatsia japonica*, a very architectural plant with its huge, deep green, shiny foliage, would make a good background too. If you have an acid soil a group of camellias, with their deep green, shiny, evergreen foliage, would make a handsome background for a light-coloured container.

At one time a British supplier was offering blue-glazed Chinese terracotta pots, imitations of products made during the Sung Dynasty (960 – 1280 AD). They were very plain and deep navy blue in colour. If you can find one of these, or something similar, you would have a marvellous item for a focal point in a Chinese or Japanese-style garden. There seems to be a trend towards gardens in the Oriental style, particularly among owners of modern town gardens. They are laid out very simply, not over-planted and, of course, rely on attractive ornaments as well as distinctive plants for creating interest and atmosphere.

Before leaving modern town gardens I should say that containers in classical styles are also often used as focal points: for example, Florentine urns and pots. Combining old with new in this way does seem to work, so do not be put off classical styles just because you live in contemporary surroundings.

However, in an informal rural or semi-rural garden, or the gardens of period houses, the classical styles really come into their own. Highly decorated urns and vases can be made to nestle attractively among shrubs and other plants. Again, do make sure that light-coloured containers have a suitably dark background.

In a country garden this might be an old yew hedge (*Taxus baccata*) with very deep blackish green foliage. Or it could be a laurel hedge (*Prunus laurocerasus*) with large, glossy, deep green foliage. Or maybe you have a group of dark-leaved shrubs which would make a good setting for a container. If you are starting from scratch, consider a group of shrubs such as laurustinus (*Viburnum tinus*), or rosemary (*Rosmarinus officinalis*) both of which have dark evergreen foliage. A bay (*Laurus nobilis*) has attractive aromatic foliage and, grown as an informal shrub, would also make a good background for a focal point.

Warm, orangy, terracotta containers can make delightful focal points in country gardens (Fig. 3). Containers of all kinds can be bought in this material, from classical urns and vases to pots, particularly the fancy or decorated pots in the style of Florentine, Venetian, Minoan and Tuscan earthenware. Traditional English pots are plain, and perhaps not so suitable as ornaments, but they can be ideal for planting for a wide range of subjects.

If you have a deep pocket, why not consider lead containers, which make superb focal points in country and period-style gardens? You can obtain copies of classical designs that come in the form of urns, vases and rectangular or hexagonal cisterns. Lead containers are generally rather small and therefore better suited to the small garden. It is possible, of course, to buy antique lead containers from specialist suppliers or antique dealers.

Of course, terracotta and lead are rather dark colours and so need a light-coloured background. In a country garden this might be a mellow, old stone wall, or maybe a wall of yellow brick. Otherwise create a suitable background with light-coloured foliage plants – perhaps choosing from the huge range of silver- or grey-leaved plants like artemisias, santolinas, lavenders or ornamental grasses such as helictotrichon. The white-striped gardener's garters grass, *Phalaris arundinacea* 'Picta', makes a superb background for terracotta containers. The focal point can be allowed to nestle among the plants but make sure they do not obscure it.

Fig. 3 A terracotta container, such as this bowl and pedestal, preferably in a warm, orangy colour, makes a delightful focal point in a country garden, especially if backed with light-coloured foliage plants such as green and white striped grasses (shown here are *Glyceria maxima* 'Variegata' [left] and *Phalaris arundinacea* 'Picta').

FOR COURTYARDS AND PATIOS

Ornamental containers are ideal for decorating courtyards. The definition of a courtyard is an area enclosed by walls (or buildings) but open to the sky. In warm countries, where the courtyard is more popular, it is used as a cool, shady place to sit, away from the heat of the day.

Traditionally courtyards are decorated with statuary, ornamental containers, pools and fountains. Statuary and containers can be as elaborate as desired and ornate classical styles of urns, vases and pots can be used. Stone, or simulated stone, containers may be more appropriate for a courtyard where subtle or neutral colours are called for. We are aiming for a 'cool', restful atmosphere.

Courtyards are sometimes paved with marble, especially so in Mediterranean countries, so why not consider square or rectangular planters made of marble? These would certainly provide elegance in any courtyard.

White-glazed clay bell pots would also help to create the right atmosphere in a courtyard. They can be used out of doors – although it might be better to take them inside for the winter if you live in an area subjected to hard winters. They look equally good indoors where they can be used as containers for potted plants. Lead containers such as cisterns and urns would also be a good choice for courtyards.

Of course you may want to plant some of your courtyard containers, particularly marble planters and the larger glazed pots. Large-leaved foliage plants would be a good choice like *Fatsia japonica*; the hardy palm, *Trachycarpus fortunei*; and hostas or plantain lilies. The oleander, *Nerium oleander*, with pink or white flowers

In this large garden an unusual copper container has been used to draw the eye to a particular part. It is planted with fuchsias and pelargoniums.

What a superb focal point for a large garden – a huge copper tub planted with standard fuchsias which give colour throughout the summer.

Fig. 4 In a large garden with a terrace or patio surrounded with stone balustrades, the pillars could be topped with ornate stone urns, which may or may not be planted, according to taste.

in summer, is a good container plant but is tender and needs to be protected from frosts, which means over-wintering it indoors or in a greenhouse. Another attractive flowering plant for courtyard containers is the white arum lily or *Zantedeschia aethiopica*. It also has bold foliage. Hardy ferns of all kinds could be grown in containers. None of these plants will actually hide the containers so you can still enjoy the latter for their own sake.

The patio will probably feature mainly planted containers, rather than urns, vases, tubs, etc, used as ornaments in their own right. However, large patios and terraces are sometimes surrounded with stone balustrades. The entrance to the terrace or patio, which may be by means of steps, is traditionally flanked by stone

pillars each of which is topped with an ornate stone urn, which may or may not be planted, according to taste (Fig. 4). There may also be stone pillars at intervals along the balustrade and these, too, traditionally support stone urns. Bear in mind that such a patio or terrace is really only suitable for large gardens – in a small garden it can look rather ostentatious.

FRAMING WITH CONTAINERS

Containers can be used for framing certain features of the garden and house. Pairs of identical containers are used for this purpose. For instance, many people flank the front door of their house, or porch, with distinctive containers. With a modern house, usually something fairly plain is called for, such as large English terracotta pots, or concrete or simulated stone planters. Invariably one will want to plant these: clipped bay trees look good, perhaps trained as pyramids, or maybe each container could be planted with a pyramid-shaped conifer.

The front door of the country cottage could be flanked with terracotta pots or even with oak half barrels, suitably varnished and with the rings painted black. Each of these could contain a topiary specimen in yew (*Taxus baccata*) or box (*Buxus sempervirens*) – very appropriate for a cottage garden.

Steps, such as those leading to a terrace, patio or sunken garden, could be flanked in a similar way with containers. Gates, too, could have twin containers on each side, as could garden arches.

3

AROUND THE HOUSE

Some containers are ideal for decorating the house, including window boxes, hanging baskets and other pendulous containers, and wall-mounted pots and baskets. Colour can be brought to balconies in the same way, and additionally with lightweight tubs, pots, troughs, etc.

WINDOW BOXES

Window boxes are available in various materials, including terracotta, which I consider is an ideal choice for cottages and perhaps period-style houses. Window boxes are also available in lead, in traditional styles, and again are a good choice for period and country houses. Very elegant marble window boxes are more suited to city houses and courtyards.

However, the more usual material used for making window boxes is wood. For the modern house choose a smart contemporary style, perhaps painted to match the colour of the house. For a country cottage a more rustic style would be appropriate, perhaps stained a natural wood colour such as dark oak. Do ensure you use a coloured horticultural wood preservative in this instance, to avoid any possible risk of plant damage.

Window boxes are also available in plastic, in various designs, and such a modern material is perhaps best suited to the contemporary home.

On the other hand, you may prefer to make your own window boxes from wood, in which case they will exactly fit the windowsills of your house. There is

no doubt that oak is the most durable wood for window boxes, but western red cedar can also be used. Window boxes must be sufficiently deep if they are not to dry out rapidly and I would therefore suggest a minimum depth of 25 cm (10 in). If you have very wide windows, say around 1.8 m (6 ft), it may be better to construct two 90 cm (3 ft) boxes so that installation and removal are very much easier. The boxes must, of course, be securely fixed to the walls with suitable brackets – black or white wrought-iron brackets are attractive.

Window boxes can be installed on the tops of balcony walls and here it is even more important to make sure they are really well secured to the walls with suitable brackets. Also, it may be advisable to place drip trays under the boxes to catch excess water.

Planting schemes

If you have attractive looking boxes it is rather pointless hiding them under masses of trailing plants. Instead plant them with upright bushy plants. Of course, cheap-looking plastic kinds are better completely hidden by trailers, as generally they are not aesthetically pleasing.

Plants will have to be chosen and arranged with special care if the boxes are placed in front of windows. Tall plants will obviously cut down the amount of light reaching the rooms of the house, but nevertheless some tall plants will be needed to give variation in height, so place them at each end of a box. In the centre

Pairs of identical containers are often used for flanking steps. These beautiful terracotta pots in a traditional style contain standard conifers underplanted with trailing plants.

In this garden pairs of stylish terracotta pots are used to 'frame' a formal garden pool. They are planted with pelargoniums and grey-leaved helichrysum.

of the box arrange low-growing plants and in front of these use trailers to cascade over the edge. Such an arrangement gives a pleasing, well-balanced effect.

If the box is on top of a balcony wall you will not be faced with the problem of reduced light in the rooms, so you can arrange plants in a triangular formation – tall plants in the centre, grading down to each end with smaller plants. Again trailers can be planted at the front of the box, ideally in front of the small plants to create a well-balanced effect.

Always consider the amount of sun and shade. There are plenty of plants available which are suitable for both situations, as described below. It is safe to say that all the plants recommended for shade would do equally well in sun, but sun-lovers will do poorly in shade, making weak growth and not flowering well. If the site is particularly windy it is best to avoid trailing plants as these are liable to be whipped around and damaged by the wind.

Backgrounds must also be taken into consideration when planting window boxes, or the plants may not show to advantage. If the background is rather cluttered or confusing then it is a good idea to choose plants (such as spring or summer bedding) in one colour, rather than mixed colours, as you will find the flowers show up much better. Mixed colours, as often found in bedding plants, need a plain background. You may wish to match colours of plants with the house colours to give a co-ordinated effect. For instance, if the colour scheme of your house is green and white you could, perhaps, create a planting scheme with white flowers and attractive green-foliage plants.

One often sees very complicated planting schemes in window boxes but these are not always very effective: the use of many different plants can look over-fussy. Better to aim for simple planting schemes using only one or two different kinds of plants, or one or two colours, ideally to match the house. This is particularly important for modern town houses. Window boxes on a country cottage can, if desired, be a riot of different colours, in keeping with the very informal, casual planting of the garden. Make sure that the window boxes are set against a plain background.

PERMANENT PLANTS

You may not want to be bothered, nor indeed have the time, to continually replant window boxes with seasonal bedding plants. Therefore why not opt for permanent plants? These need little attention the year round, apart from regular watering, although eventually some of them may become too large and will need to be lifted and replaced with smaller specimens.

For a country setting why not try a box of miniature roses which flower throughout summer, perhaps with trailing periwinkle (*Vinca minor* varieties) trailing over the edge for spring colour? A scheme for shade could consist of small evergreen foliage shrubs like the dwarf edging box, *Buxus sempervirens* 'Suffruticosa', *Skimmia reevesiana* with white flowers in spring and red berries throughout winter, and an edging of trailing *Lysimachia nummularia* with yellow flowers in summer.

Perhaps in a more modern or formal setting dwarf conifers could be used, like *Juniperus communis* 'Compressa', a tiny grey cone; *Chamaecyparis lawsoniana* 'Ellwoodii', grey foliage; and yellow-tinted *C. 1.*

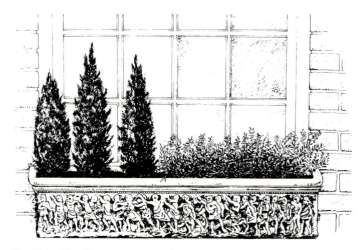

Fig. 5 An idea for a permanent planting scheme in a terracotta window box, in a modern or formal setting: a group of the tiny Noah's ark juniper, *Juniperis communis* 'Compressa', with varieties of winter-flowering heather, *Erica herbacea* (syn. *E. carnea*). Some varieties of heather have golden foliage to create year-round interest.

'Ellwood's Gold'. Among these could be planted varieties of winter-flowering heather, *Erica herbacea* (syn. *E. carnea*) (Fig. 5). Some varieties have golden foliage to create additional interest.

Other useful foliage shrubs include the variegated varieties of *Euonymus fortunei*, like 'Emerald and Gold' with bright gold variegated foliage, ideal for shade; the trailing varieties of ivy, *Hedera helix*, with variegated or plain green foliage, all shade-lovers; and the variegated spotted laurel, *Aucuba japonica* 'Variegata', suitable for shade. Taking partial shade is the cabbage tree, *Cordyline australis*, with sword-like leaves, ideal for giving height to a planting scheme.

Small foliage shrubs for sun include dwarf lavenders, like *Lavandula angustifolia* 'Munstead', and the silvery cotton lavender, *Santolina chamaecyparissus*.

Small flowering shrubs suitable for window boxes include several hebes or shrubby veronicas, like *H. pinguifolia* 'Pagei' with grey foliage and white flowers, and the violet 'Carl Teschner', both flowering profusely in summer. Full sun needed. *Pernettya mucronata* 'Bell's

Fig. 6 Temporary plants, like these winter-flowering pansies, can be planted among permanent subjects in a window box. The shrub in the centre is the variegated evergreen, *Aucuba japonica* 'Variegata', and those at each end variegated varieties of *Euonymus fortunei*, also evergreen.

Seedling' is grown for its deep red autumn and winter berries, while the dwarf evergreen azaleas, like the Kurume hybrids, produce masses of flowers in early summer. Both of these must have acid or lime-free compost and they do well in shade or partial shade.

Among these shrubs can be planted miniature bulbs like daffodils and snowdrops, both of which are suitable for shade; and, for a sunny spot, crocuses (especially *Crocus chrysanthus* varieties), scillas, chionodoxas and muscari.

TEMPORARY PLANTS

Temporary plants include summer bedding and other tender plants, and spring bedding plants and bulbs. There is no need to devote window boxes entirely to temporary plants: dwarf conifers and evergreen shrubs, and permanent trailing plants, can still be used and they associate well with bedding plants and bulbs, which can be planted among them. The shrubs and conifers would be used as single specimen plants in this instance. Try winter-flowering pansies, or for spring colour polyanthus, coloured primroses or double daisies (*Bellis perennis*) around shrubs like *Euonymus fortunei* or *Aucuba japonica* 'Variegata', these giving much-needed height to the scheme (Fig. 6). All of these can be grown in a shady spot.

There is no doubt that summer bedding and other tender plants are the most popular subjects for window boxes, no doubt because they produce so much colour over a very long period – from early summer until the frosts start in the autumn. Although the majority need plenty of sun, nevertheless there are several plants that grow and flower well in shade. These include the wax begonia (*Begonia semperflorens*) and, for trailing over the edge, pendulous tuberous begonias. Also suitable for shade are the bedding impatiens or busy lizzie; pansies; bush and trailing fuchsias; spider plants (*Chlorophytum comosum* 'Variegatum') grown for their green and white striped foliage; asparagus fern (*Asparagus densiflorus* 'Sprengeri'), another useful foliage pot plant for boxes; the bell flower (*Campanula isophylla*); the variegated ground ivy (*Glechoma hederacea* 'Variegata'); and the bedding calceolaria

Here a dark green hedge makes the perfect background for light-coloured tiered bowls which create an excellent focal point. The bed and containers are planted with summer bedding plants.

A terracotta urn in classical style. Used as focal points, such containers could be left unplanted but here pelargoniums and trailing ivies have been used to good effect.

(*Calceolaria rugosa*). The chlorophytum, asparagus, campanula and glechoma can be kept from year to year, if overwintered in frost-free conditions.

Summer bedding and other tender plants which need plenty of sun include pelargoniums: the bushy zonal varieties for giving height to the centre of the box, the ivy-leaved varieties for trailing over the edge. Of the latter, do not use the variegated-leaved varieties as their flowers are sparingly produced. Really the best for flowering are the new Swiss balcony 'geraniums' which produce cascades of blooms all summer. Other popular trailing or spreading plants include lobelia; the grey-leaved tender perennial, *Helichrysum petiolatum*; small-flowered multiflora petunias and verbenas.

Bushier plants include white daisy-flowered marguerites (*Chrysanthemum frutescens*); ageratum; coleus for their coloured foliage; annual pinks (*Dianthus chinensis* varieties); dwarf African marigolds like the 'Inca' series; and even dwarf sweet peas, which are hardy annuals, best raised under glass in spring. To replace fading summer bedding plants in the autumn consider the early-flowering charm chrysanthemums. These would have to be pot grown elsewhere and could then be plunged, in their pots, in the boxes as they come into flower.

Again with summer displays, do try to keep the planting schemes simple. You will find the effect more pleasing than a kaleidoscope of colours. Summer bedding can be supported with permanent plants in the boxes, such as trailing ivies at the front. Schemes like wax begonias with chlorophytum; pelargoniums with helichrysum; and African marigolds with marguerites are the sort of simple schemes I have in mind. What better for cottage window sills than boxfuls of dwarf sweet peas or impatiens? Once again, if you want a co-ordinated effect, choose colours to match the house.

HANGING BASKETS

Hanging baskets can be chosen to suit the style of the house, although if well planted they may be com-pletely hidden. Nevertheless one has a choice of trad-itional and modern designs. Traditional hanging baskets are made from galvanized wire and certainly look most at home around period-style houses and country cottages. They have the advantage that plants can be planted through the wires, so providing a ball of colour. There is a supplier offering very modern-looking wire-mesh baskets which would look good in a contemporary setting, although the mesh is small so you cannot actually plant through it.

Modern moulded plastic baskets would be appropriate for a contemporary setting and some of them have built-in drip trays, particularly useful if they are to be used on balconies. Hanging terracotta containers are very attractive and look good in any setting.

Make sure you buy the largest possible hanging baskets or containers as very small ones dry out rapidly. A good size is 30 cm (12 in) in diameter, which should also have adequate depth.

There are plenty of places to site hanging baskets, but for obvious reasons one should avoid windy sites. They can be placed in sun or shade, for there are plants suitable for both positions. Fix them to the house walls (ideally with ornamental wrought-iron brackets), in porches and to the ceiling of balconies. Make sure the baskets are not too high or you may have difficulty with watering, which often has to be done on a daily basis in warm weather, although there are available long watering lances which are attached to a hosepipe.

Planting schemes

As with window boxes, simple planting schemes are the most effective, even going for single subjects to create real impact. Single-subject baskets are also easier to plant and do not result in that 'over-fussy' effect of many plants arranged together.

Choice of colour schemes will be influenced by backgrounds. If the background is cluttered and fussy then go for plant varieties of one colour. If the background is perfectly plain, such as a rendered wall painted white or cream, then you can certainly use varieties in mixed colours. If the baskets are in shade you will need to use light-coloured plants as they will show up much better than dark colours. For instance, use pale pink or white begonias or impatiens, or yellow pansies. If you have traditional wire hanging baskets then certainly plant through the wires around the sides, as well as in the top, as this will result in a complete ball of colour.

On the whole, plants of a trailing or semi-trailing habit are used for baskets, although there is no reason why a more bushy specimen should not be planted in the centre if desired. The most popular basket plants for summer colour include pendulous begonias and fuchsias (suitable for shade); verbena; lobelia (takes light shade); *Calceolaria* 'Sunshine' (takes light shade); multiflora petunias (such as the 'Resisto' series); and ivy-leaved pelargoniums (not variegated-leaved varieties).

More unusual choices for baskets include nasturtium 'Alaska' with variegated foliage, ideal for cottage gardens, the seeds being sown direct in the baskets; dwarf sweet peas like 'Knee-Hi' and 'Bijou', also a good choice for cottages; and the black-eyed susan, *Thunbergia alata*, a half-hardy annual.

For autumn colour try some baskets of charm chrysanthemums, although make sure they are not subjected to hard frosts. These could be grown in pots and planted in baskets in autumn as they are coming into flower.

Of course you may not have the time, nor the desire, to plant baskets with temporary seasonal plants, but there are quite a few permanent plants which are suitable. I have tried planting baskets with winter-flowering heathers, varieties of *Erica herbacea* (*E. carnea*), which has proved successful. Varieties of *Vinca minor* or periwinkle produce their starry blue, purple or white flowers in spring and are suitable for shade or partial shade. Also thriving in shade are the small-leaved ivies, varieties of *Hedera helix* with variegated or green foliage. Miniature spring-flowering bulbs could be planted with these (Fig. 7).

Creeping Jenny or *Lysimachia nummularia* is a charming trailing perennial for shade or sun, with yellow

Fig. 7 Many permanent plants are suited to hanging baskets. Here, blue grape hyacinths or muscari (miniature bulbs) contrast, in the spring, with variegated ivy.

flowers in summer. Even more colourful is the golden-leaved variety.

Temporary shade-tolerant plants for winter and spring colour include winter-flowering pansies, such as the 'Universal' strain, double daisies or bellis, and coloured primroses. All too often baskets are empty during these seasons, but there is no need for this.

WALL POTS

Half-round ornamental pots are available which are fixed directly to walls, wherever desired, and they can

29

This stone bowl on a plinth, in classical style, shows up really well against a dark green yew hedge. Grey-leaved helichrysum and pelargoniums make a tasteful summer display.

These wall baskets are being used in a similar way to conventional hanging baskets, having been attractively planted with pendulous begonias for summer colour.

be used in the same way as hanging baskets (Fig. 8). Most are produced in terracotta but if you want something rather special then lead wall pots are available in traditional styles. Details of siting and planting as for hanging baskets, above.

BALCONY CONTAINERS

Window boxes, hanging containers and wall pots are admirable for balconies, but the balcony gardener will also want some suitable containers for the floor. Here

Fig. 8 Wall pots, which are fixed directly to walls, are extremely useful as they enable colourful or interesting plants to be positioned anywhere on the house. They are available in lead and, more often, in terracotta, as shown here. Ivies, ferns, ivy-leaved pelargoniums and many other plants with a trailing or arching habit are suitable for these kinds of container.

one should choose lightweight tubs, urns, pots, troughs, etc and also use a lightweight compost for filling them – the all-peat potting composts are ideal.

A wide range of containers is available in plastic and fibreglass and although some may not be as attractive as those in, say, reconstituted stone or terracotta, nevertheless they can be well hidden with trailing plants.

Planting ideas will be found in Chapter 4.

4

COLOUR ON THE PATIO

One of the most popular parts of a garden for planted containers is the patio. Here one can use the wide range of tubs, urns, vases, pots, troughs and bowls; again, as emphasized earlier, choosing styles to suit the style of the house and garden. Also, the plants used should be appropriate for the particular setting: for instance, bold, modern-looking kinds for the contemporary patio, olde-worlde kinds for the informal cottage garden.

With a good collection of containers one can, by careful choice of plants, ensure colour and interest all the year round, using a combination of permanent plants and temporary kinds like spring, summer and autumn bedding. Provided you are able to, containers can be moved around to give different effects at various times of the year. For instance, many people like to plant containers with spring bedding plants such as wallflowers, forget-me-nots and double daisies, plus spring bulbs. But these look decidedly dreary throughout the autumn and winter and would be better placed in a spare part of the garden, out of site, until the plants are coming into flower, when the containers can be moved on to the patio. Tender summer bedding plants could be planted in containers under glass, to get them established, and again they could be moved out on to the patio when in full bloom – ideally, after hardening off in a cold frame. Permanent tender plants can be placed on the patio for the summer, perhaps to give a Mediterranean or sub-tropical effect, and moved back under cover (indoors or into a frost-free greenhouse or conservatory) before the autumn frosts commence. In very cold parts of the country many permanent, nor-

mally hardy plants would be better over-wintered in a cool, frost-free greenhouse or conservatory as they are liable to suffer outside in severe winters. (A useful piece of equipment for moving containers is the two-wheeled sack trolly – rather like the trollies used by railway porters.)

It is important to choose containers of suitable size for plants. Depth is especially important to allow plants to root deeply and to prevent rapid drying out of the compost. With the majority of containers available the depth is perfectly adequate – it is, of course, generally in proportion to the diameter of the container. There are some containers, though, whose depth is not in proportion to the diameter and these are the modern shallow concrete bowls. However, these are widely used in modern settings, mainly for bedding plants which do not mind dryish conditions, but a close eye should be kept on the compost as it can rapidly dry out in warm conditions.

So what is a suitable size for patio containers? Whether you want to grow temporary or permanent plants, we are thinking in terms of containers with a diameter of at least 30 cm (12 in). These will hold several bedding plants, or single small shrubs, perennials, conifers, etc. But you can have more effective bedding displays with larger containers – say with diameters of 45–60 cm (18–24 in). These sizes of container are also recommended for larger permanent plants like shrubs, conifers, small trees and so on. If containers are much larger than this they really cease to be portable and come in the category of permanent 'planters', which are discussed in Chapter 5.

The walls of this house are colourful from bottom to top as various types of container have been colourfully planted, with climbing roses and nasturtiums adding to the effect.

Wall-mounted containers are invaluable as they can be used to provide colour wherever desired around the house. These contain pelargoniums, fuchsias and lobelia.

TEMPORARY PLANTS

Temporary plants are used to give seasonal colour on the patio and include the obvious spring, summer and autumn bedding plants, as well as tender shrubs, perennials and succulents, and hardy annuals.

Modern formal settings

In a modern formal setting modern, simple containers are the most appropriate. For example, concrete or reconstituted-stone tubs, large plain pots in orange or buff terracotta and large shallow concrete bowls. Modern concrete, reconstituted stone or terracotta troughs are also very attractive in such a setting.

TENDER SHRUBS AND PERENNIALS
Although tender shrubs and perennials are grown permanently in containers, they have to be moved into a frost-free greenhouse or conservatory, or indoors, for the winter. They are useful for giving a sub-tropical effect on the patio throughout the summer and can be grouped with colourful summer bedding plants.

The oleander, *Nerium oleander*, is a Mediterranean shrub which makes a good tub plant. It has lanceolate, leathery, evergreen foliage and red, pink, cream or white flowers in summer and autumn. It makes quite a large shrub and needs plenty of sun.

Citrus fruits are excellent tub plants and eventually make fairly large shrubs. They are grown as bushes or dwarf pyramids. Most people like to grow the various oranges, such as the sweet orange, *Citrus sinensis*, and the Seville orange, *C. aurantium*. The white flowers are deliciously scented. Plenty of sun needed.

Abutilon striatum 'Thompsonii' is a striking foliage shrub with large yellow-mottled leaves and orange flowers. It makes a fairly large shrub for a sunny spot. Sometimes small plants are used as temporary bedding plants to give foliage interest among flowering kinds.

An extremely useful tub plant is the New Zealand cabbage palm, *Cordyline australis*, with very long, narrow, greyish green leaves. It will take sun or partial shade and makes an imposing single specimen, or very often small plants are used as a centrepiece for tubs of summer bedding plants.

The aromatic, grey-leaved *Eucalyptus globulus* is a fast grower and will quickly become too large for a container, but it can be used for a few years to help create a sub-tropical effect on the summer patio.

Of the succulent perennials, the century plant, *Agave americana* 'Marginata', is a striking subject for the modern patio with its rosette of stiff sword-shaped leaves edged with yellow. It is slow growing and needs plenty of sun.

Small pots of *Echeveria glauca* dotted among tubs of summer bedding plants look attractive. This plant has rosettes of greyish foliage and is also a sun lover.

Indian shot, or *Canna* × *generalis*, is a tender perennial which grows from fleshy rhizomes. The plant becomes dormant in winter and is rested in dry compost. It is restarted into growth in early spring by repotting, resuming watering and increasing temperature. The bold foliage may be green, bronze or purple and in summer spikes of exotic, highly colourful lily-like flowers are produced, creating a truly tropical effect in a sunny spot.

ANNUALS FOR FOLIAGE EFFECT
There are several tender plants which are treated as annuals (discarded at the end of the season) which can be used for foliage effect on the patio during the summer. They can be grown on their own or used as centrepieces in tubs of summer bedding plants. The castor-oil plant, *Ricinus communis*, creates a tropical touch with its huge palmate leaves, which may be plain green or, in some of the newer varieties, heavily flushed with bronze. It likes the sun and is raised from seed in early spring – as indeed are all plants recommended here.

Coleus, with their multi-coloured foliage, are all too often thought of only in terms of greenhouse or conservatory pot plants, yet they are successfully grown outside during the summer – they can be used among summer bedding plants if desired, or mass planted in containers of their own.

Among the most highly coloured foliage plants are the amaranthus, particularly some of the newer strains like 'Flaming Fountains', 'Illumination' and 'Red Fox', with red or multicoloured foliage.

SUMMER BEDDING PLANTS

The contemporary patio and its surrounding architecture call out for brightly coloured summer bedding plants. But this does not necessarily mean a kaleidoscope of colours creating an over-fussy effect, which is perhaps better for the patio around the country cottage. As with window boxes, you may find that using single or perhaps two contrasting subjects creates more impact, especially if the colours are co-ordinated with those of the house. Indeed, some of the ideas for window boxes, outlined in Chapter 3, could well be used for patio troughs (in reconstituted stone or terracotta). Patio tubs are often planted with tallish subjects in the centre surrounded with trailing plants.

I like a simple mix of flowering and foliage plants, such as red or orange zonal pelargoniums with silver-leaved *Senecio cineraria*; or bush fuchsias with the grey-leaved *Helichrysum petiolatum*. The popular wax begonias, *Begonia semperflorens*, with pink, red or white flowers, actually look very good with trailing small-leaved ivies – an ideal combination for a shady part of the patio (Fig. 9).

Also suitable for shade are the bedding varieties of busy lizzie, or impatiens, and the mimulus hybrids. I prefer to use these alone in containers and generally plant them in strawberry-type terracotta pots (the ones with holes in the sides for planting) which results in domes of colour.

Dwarf bedding dahlias are excellent for tubs and troughs, either single or mixed colours. They flower throughout summer and into the autumn. Petunias are also popular plants for tubs, troughs, etc where they are usually allowed to cascade over the edges, the centre of the container having taller, bushier plants such as zonal pelargoniums. The small-flowered multiflora petunias are best as they are more rain-resistant than the large-flowered kinds.

Very well suited to shallow concrete bowls are bed-

Fig. 9 A summer scheme for a modern patio, using concrete tubs. Flower colour is provided in one tub by the wax or bedding begonia, *Begonia semperflorens*; this being surrounded by trailing small-leaved ivies which can stay in the container the year round. Contrasting foliage is provided by the century plant, *Agave americana* 'Marginata' (*left*) and by the castor-oil plant, *Ricinus communis*.

ding plants which revel in hot dry conditions. These include the daisy-flowered gazania hybrids, in shades of yellow, orange, pink, etc, and the multi-coloured Livingstone daisy, *Mesembryanthemum criniflorum*. You could provide height in the centre of the bowl with a century plant, *Agave americana* 'Marginata'.

If you need autumn colour on the patio consider some tubs of charm chrysanthemums with myriad small flowers in various colours. These could be planted in the containers in early summer, relegated to a spare part of the garden for the summer and moved on to the patio when in flower.

The front entrance to this house has been considerably brightened up with a traditional wooden tub and hanging baskets overflowing with fuchsias and petunias.

If the background is plain, wall containers and hanging baskets can be a kaleidoscope of colours, provided, for example, by summer bedding plants like begonias, impatiens, lobelia and helichrysum.

SPRING BEDDING PLANTS AND BULBS

These are planted in the autumn and as they are by no means attractive until they come into flower they should, ideally, be stored in a spare part of the garden until spring.

The usual spring bedding plants for tubs, etc, are double daisies, wallflowers, the Siberian wallflower and forget-me-nots. Dwarf spring bulbs can be combined with any of these, such as the greigii and kaufmanniana tulips and hyacinths.

You might like to consider, too, the winter-flowering pansies, like the 'Universal' strain – these really do flower in winter, often peeping through a covering of snow.

An observation I have made with bedding plants in containers (whether summer or spring kinds) is that a better effect is created if the containers are grouped together, rather than scattered around singly.

Cottage-garden and country settings

Here more traditional containers like wooden tubs and troughs, and half barrels, make suitable containers. Urns, pots and vases in classical styles look good, too, and particularly in association with period-style houses.

Choose plants to suit the style of the garden. Often old-fashioned plants and flowers look more at home on the patio of a country cottage.

BEDDING PLANTS

What better for a country cottage than tubs full of ornamental tobacco or nicotiana? Choose good modern strains, particularly those which are scented in the evening like 'Evening Fragrance' and 'Nicki Formula Mixed'. As these come in mixed colours I feel that no other plants are needed.

Ivy-leaf pelargoniums will also make a good display and could be combined with that favourite cottage-garden plant, heliotrope.

Other summer bedding plants that deserve a place on the cottage patio are ageratum, useful for edging tubs, trailing lobelia, *Nemesia strumosa*, petunias and verbena hybrids. Annual pinks and carnations are considered 'essential' cottage-garden plants, as are violas and pansies.

It is more appropriate in this setting to have a glorious mixture of plants in the tubs and troughs, so do not be afraid to combine several kinds of plants. Spring bedding plants and bulbs can include all of those recommended above.

HARDY ANNUALS

Some of the hardy annuals are recommended for cottage-garden tubs and troughs, sown direct where they are to flower. The pot marigold or *Calendula officinalis* should be in every cottage garden, and this is true also of nasturtiums. Choose the dwarf bushy kinds for containers, rather than the climbing types. Have tubs full of dwarf sweet peas, too, but make sure they never go short of moisture.

PERMANENT PLANTS

There is a surprisingly wide range of permanent plants for containers, including shrubs, conifers, small trees, climbers, roses and hardy perennials. The woody plants – the shrubs, trees, conifers and climbers – provide a 'framework' and background for containers of temporary plants and they help to provide an established, mature atmosphere. One can create pleasing seasonal groups, too, such as spring-flowering shrubs with spring bedding plants and bulbs (Fig. 10). Containers of colourful summer bedding plants could be given a background of evergreen foliage shrubs or mixed with roses and hardy perennials for contrast in colour, form and texture.

Containers for most of these subjects must, of course, be sufficiently large – 30 cm (12 in) diameter for small shrubs, etc, and for perennials; and 45 – 60 cm (18 – 24 in) in diameter for larger specimens. Very

Fig. 10 Permanent plants in tubs can be used in seasonal groups. Here a camellia is surrounded by terracotta urns containing daffodils and tulips – a most pleasing combination for the spring patio.

important is adequate depth. Generally, the plants recommended here look best in tubs or large pots, rather than troughs and containers such as narrow-necked urns.

Permanent plants make for labour-saving gardening, so this may be important, and furthermore they really do help to ensure year-round interest and colour on the patio.

Modern formal settings

Again, plants should suit the setting, and containers, too, as discussed earlier. So let us start with plants that can be used to furnish patios in contemporary settings.

SHRUBS

I suggest a combination of flowering and foliage shrubs. Also specimens clipped to regular shapes, such as bay (*Laurus nobilis*), box (*Buxus sempervirens*) and hollies (ilex) trained into pyramids, standards, etc, which make useful accent specimens on the patio – perhaps to frame a door or steps.

Other foliage shrubs include the 'architectural' *Fatsia japonica*, with large, palmate, glossy evergreen leaves which make a good background for more colourful plants. It takes semi-shade. Equally dramatic is *Aralia elata* with massive deciduous compound leaves.

Pieris formosa forrestii is really grown for its foliage, although in spring it produces trusses of white bell-shaped flowers. The young leaves of this evergreen are spectacular – glowing red in colour. It needs lime-free compost, shelter and ideally partial shade.

The gold-splashed leaves of *Elaeagnus pungens* 'Maculata' will provide a bright splash of colour all the year round, as will those of *Euonymus japonicus* 'Aureopictus'. Here the leaves are golden, edged with green. It will take partial shade. Small-growing euonymus are the *E. fortunei* varieties, which also take shade, like golden-variegated 'Emerald and Gold'.

Some of the small or slow-growing hollies make excellent tub plants, including the silver hedgehog holly, *Ilex aquifolium* 'Ferox Argentea', whose very spiny leaves are edged with white. The dwarf *I. crenata* 'Golden Gem' has tiny oval, golden leaves.

Ivies are shade-lovers and extremely useful for the edges of containers, when they will cascade down the sides. The small-leaved *Hedera helix* varieties are best, including such well-known kinds as 'Adam', white-edged leaves; 'Buttercup', deep yellow foliage; 'Glacier', silvery grey; and 'Goldheart', yellow-splashed leaves. The plain green ivies like 'Caenwoodiana', 'Green Ripple', 'Ivalace' and 'Sagittifolia'

One of the most popular parts of a garden for planted containers is the patio. Here, traditional designs have been used in a period setting.

Raised beds as well as other ornamental containers can ensure plenty of colour on and around a patio if generously planted with bedding and other summer flowers.

make an excellent foil for brightly coloured flowers, such as summer bedding.

The dwarf viburnum, *V. davidii*, has large, deep green, deeply veined leaves and, if several plants are grown together, crops of turquoise berries.

In mild sheltered areas it is worth growing in a tub the hardy palm, *Trachycarpus fortunei*, with large fan-shaped leaves and a shaggy brown trunk. It helps to create a sub-tropical effect, as do the yuccas with their sword-like foliage, such as *Y. gloriosa*, *Y. filamentosa* and its variety 'Variegata', and *Y. flaccida* 'Ivory'. These all eventually produce spikes of bell-shaped flowers.

The Japanese maples, varieties of *Acer palmatum*, are noted for their brilliant autumn leaf colour and should be grown in a sheltered, partially shaded spot. Some have purple summer foliage, such as 'Atropurpureum' and 'Dissectum Atropurpureum'.

Coming on to flowering shrubs, dwarf rhododendrons and azaleas grow well in tubs; they need lime-free compost and ideally a position in dappled or partial shade. *Rhododendron yakushimanum*, with white flowers, and its coloured hybrids, are outstanding, as are the early flowering, purple, 'Praecox', white, fragrant *R. mucronatum*, and deep red 'Elizabeth'. Dwarf evergreen azaleas like white 'Palestrina', pink 'Rosebud' and crimson 'Hinodegiri' are simply 'made' for tubs.

Camellias look good all year round with their deep green glossy foliage and produce their flowers in many shades of red, pink and also white, in late winter and spring. Varieties of *C. japonica* and *C. × williamsii* are recommended. Grow in lime-free compost in a partially shaded position, which does not receive early morning sun.

Heathers are useful for grouping around larger shrubs, especially the varieties of winter-flowering *Erica herbacea* (*E. carnea*).

Try also the dwarf laurel, *Prunus laurocerasus* 'Otto Luyken', with handsome evergreen foliage and spikes of white flowers in spring; and the dwarf evergreen *Skimmia reevesiana* with red berries in autumn/winter.

CONIFERS
Small-growing conical, globular or prostrate conifers make ideal accent plants for the formal patio. Try the following: *Chamaecyparis lawsoniana* 'Ellwoodii', a grey-green cone; *C. l.* 'Ellwood's Gold', tinged with yellow; *Chamaecyparis pisifera* 'Boulevard', a steel-blue cone; *Juniperus × media* 'Mint Julep', arching, spreading habit, rich green; and *J. × media* 'Blaauw', with partially upright branches and grey-blue foliage.

SMALL TREES
Small ornamental trees are useful for giving height and dappled shade on the patio. Try the following: *Malus floribunda*, with pale pink flowers in spring, followed by yellow fruits; *Prunus* 'Amanogawa', with pale pink cherry blossom in spring; the weeping *Pyrus salicifolia* 'Pendula' with silver willowy leaves; the golden-leaved *Robinia pseudoacacia* 'Frisia'; *Salix caprea* 'Pendula', a weeping willow with yellow catkins; and *Sorbus* 'Joseph Rock' with yellow autumn berries and good autumn foliage colour.

CLIMBERS
Climbers can be trained to patio or house walls, trellis screens or over a pergola. The large-flowered clematis hybrids look good on the modern patio, especially when combined with climbing roses. They like their roots in shade and their 'heads' in sun.

The ivies are also recommended: I have already described some varieties of *Hedera helix* (see page 41) but consider also the large-leaved, variegated *Hedera canariensis* 'Gloire de Marengo' and *H. colchica* 'Dentata Variegata'.

For autumn colour on a shady (or sunny) wall try the Virginia creeper, *Parthenocissus tricuspidata*. One of my favourite climbers for tubs is the ornamental grape vine, *Vitis* 'Brant', which looks superb growing over a pergola, bearing crops of edible black berries and displaying good autumn leaf colour. It needs plenty of sun.

ROSES
Many kinds of roses can be grown in containers. The obvious choice is the huge range of miniatures, which attain no more than 45 cm (18 in) in height, flowering

profusely in summer with tiny blooms like scaled-down versions of large-flowered (hybrid tea) and cluster-flowered (floribunda) roses.

The low-growing cluster-flowered varieties are ideal, too, for the modern patio: there are lots of varieties like 'Anna Ford', orange-red; 'Kerry Gold', deep yellow; 'Marlena', crimson; 'Regensburg', pink and white; and 'Topsi', orange-scarlet.

Small-growing climbing roses suitable for tubs include 'Aloha', salmon-pink; 'Copenhagen', deep scarlet; and 'Golden Showers', bright yellow. Try a combination of climbing roses and clematis – some stunning effects can be created.

HARDY PERENNIALS

A selection of flowering and foliage perennials will help to create contrast in shape and texture. For the modern patio try to choose distinctive or 'architectural' plants, like *Acanthus spinosus* with bold, deeply divided foliage and spikes of mauve and white flowers. Or *Agapanthus* 'Headborne Hybrids' with strap-shaped foliage and heads of lily-like flowers in shades of blue.

Euphorbia wulfenii is a stately plant that will thrive in partial shade, with greyish foliage and large heads of green-yellow flowers.

Any of the ornamental grasses are suitable for containers, useful for providing contrast in foliage shape. Suitable for shade are the lenten roses, *Helleborus orientalis*, with palmate evergreen foliage and pink, purple or white cup-shaped flowers very early in the year. The day lilies, hemerocallis hybrids, produce their lily-like flowers throughout summer and into autumn. They come in a wide range of colours. The hostas with their large, bold leaves, in many shades of green and yellow, and variegated, are essentially foliage plants but spikes of mauve, lilac or white flowers are produced in summer. There are no finer foliage plants for shade than the hostas.

Rodgersia pinnata 'Superba' has large, palmate, bronze leaves and produces pink flowers in summer. It will grow in partial shade and looks good near a pool.

If you want to create a Mediterranean atmosphere on your patio try the following perennials: *Beschorneria yuccoides* has greyish green yucca-like evergreen leaves and tall stems of red-bracted flowers; the red hot poker, *Kniphofia caulescens*, has dramatic glaucous grassy foliage and in autumn spikes of salmon-red flowers; some of the eryngiums are truly dramatic plants, like *E. agavifolium* with rosettes of spiny sword-shaped leaves, and *E. bromeliifolium* with rosettes of jagged-edged strap-shaped leaves.

The phormiums, or New Zealand flaxes, have sword-shaped evergreen leaves and the modern dwarf forms are ideally suited to containers. Try such colourful varieties as 'Cream Delight', 'Maori Sunrise', 'Sundowner' and 'Yellow Wave'. These four subjects need a warm, sunny, sheltered position and are better suited to milder parts of the country or overwintered under glass in cold areas.

DWARF BULBS

Remember that dwarf or miniature bulbs, such as muscari, chionodoxa, scilla, crocuses, miniature daffodils, snowdrops, bulbous irises, and so on can be planted permanently around shrubs, trees, climbers and roses to provide spring colour.

Cottage and country settings

The patio in the cottage or country garden calls for more informal plants, even old-fashioned kinds, to reflect the planting of the main garden.

SHRUBS

There are several flowering shrubs suited to tubs which look at home in the cottage garden, including the smaller hardy fuchsias like the *F. magellanica* varieties 'Pumila', red and violet, and 'Variegata' with cream-edged leaves and red and purple flowers. There are lots of hybrids, too, like 'Alice Hoffman' (red and white), 'Margaret' (crimson and violet), 'Mrs Popple' (red and violet) and 'Tom Thumb' (red and violet). All will take partial shade, as will the varieties of *Hydrangea macrophylla*, which have large mop-headed flowers in

Terracotta containers come in all shapes and sizes and really look at home in any situation. They contrast well with the neutral colour of paving.

On a patio a collection of containers looks best grouped together, rather than scattered around indiscriminately. This collection of terracotta ware even includes old chimney pots.

blue, pink, red or white. Use an acid compost if you want blue flowers.

The Mexican orange blossom, *Choisya ternata*, is an evergreen with handsome foliage and highly scented white flowers in spring and summer. It needs a sheltered sunny spot. Also an evergreen, with yellow-edged leaves, is *Daphne odora* 'Aureomarginata' with very fragrant red-purple flowers in spring. Needs full sun.

Some of the smaller hebes make good tub plants in a sheltered sunny spot and have evergreen, often elegant foliage, as well as a profusion of flowers in summer and autumn. Of the vast range, I can particularly recommend *H. × franciscana* 'Blue Gem'; 'Marjorie', light violet and white; 'Mrs E. Tennant', light violet; and *H. rakaiensis*, white.

Many of the 'modern' conifers look ill at ease in informal gardens, but yews are a good choice. For a tub try the pillar-like Irish yew, *Taxus baccata* 'Fastigiata', which is happy in shade.

TREES

The crataegus or thorns look at home in country gardens, and for a tub I would especially recommend *Crataegus oxyacantha* 'Paul's Scarlet', with double scarlet flowers in late spring. Try also *Cotoneaster* 'Hybridus Pendulus' whose white flowers are followed by crops of red berries. It is an evergreen, and should be bought as a grafted plant on a 1.8 m (6 ft) stem, when it will make a weeping specimen.

CLIMBERS

'Old fashioned' scented climbers are called for here, like jasmines and honeysuckles. The summer jasmine, *Jasminum officinale*, has deliciously scented white flowers in summer. The yellow blooms of the winter jasmine, *J. nudiflorum*, are not scented, but it is well worth growing for winter colour, particularly on a shaded wall.

The honeysuckles like their heads in the sun but their roots shaded. A good scented one is the early Dutch honeysuckle, *Lonicera periclymenum* 'Belgica', with yellow and reddish-purple flowers in spring and summer.

ROSES

Especially suitable for cottage-garden tubs are the polyantha roses, low-growing shrubs varying in height from 30 – 90 cm (12 – 36 in) and producing clusters of small blooms throughout summer and into autumn. Try 'Baby Faurax', pale violet; 'Ellen Poulsen', rose-pink; 'Little White Pet', double, white; 'Paul Crampel', orange-scarlet; 'The Fairy', rose-pink; and 'Yvonne Rabier', double, white.

'Ballerina' is a small modern shrub rose but looks superb in the cottage garden over a very long period, with its huge clusters of small, pink, white-eyed flowers.

Of the climbing roses, there is an old China rose (introduced 1839), called 'Pom-Pon de Paris', which attains no more than 1.8 m (6 ft) in height and bears tiny but well-shaped pink flowers in the summer. A couple of feet taller is 'Crimson Shower', a summer-flowering rambler with small crimson rosette-like flowers.

PERENNIALS

Some of the perennials recommended for modern patios can be used in cottage and country gardens, including hostas and hemerocallis; plus such typical cottage plants as lady's mantle, *Alchemilla mollis*, with mounds of yellow-green flowers in summer, suitable for partial shade; the shade-loving bergenias with their large leathery evergreen leaves and pink, red or white flowers in spring; the peach-leaved bellflower, *Campanula persicifolia*, with spires of blue flowers in summer, suitable for partial shade; the 'Russell Hybrid' lupins, which flower in early summer and come in many colours; and even delphinium hybrids, both tall and dwarf, with stately spires in blue, purple or white.

5

MINI-GARDENS

In large permanent (non-portable) containers like raised beds, planters, raised borders and double walls, it is somewhat easier than with smaller containers to create attractive planting schemes, for one has more space. Indeed such containers can be thought of as conventional beds when it comes to planting.

Raised beds, borders and so on can, if desired, be devoted to collections of plants, perhaps alpines or maybe lime-hating plants (especially recommended if you garden on alkaline soil and desperately want to grow such charming plants as dwarf rhododendrons, camellias, heathers and other acid-loving plants). Certainly each container can be a mini-garden.

RAISED BEDS AND PLANTERS

These terms are really synonymous and refer to large raised structures, which may be any shape desired if you build them yourself. Very often they are included as features on patios, but can be used in various parts of the garden, being particularly popular with owners of very small town gardens, as they help to create different levels in what are invariably flat sites. Large square, rectangular or circular planters can be bought, if you do not wish to construct your own; they come in various materials and are simply placed where desired on the patio.

In a very modern setting circular concrete sewer-pipe sections make excellent planters. If space permits you could, perhaps, have a group of three. The sections can be set in cobbles or granite setts and then painted with masonry paint to match the house. Make sure the base is not in very close contact with the ground for excess water must be able to escape.

If you wish to make your own beds they can be constructed from ornamental concrete walling blocks, in brick or stone finish to match the house and patio. Alternatively you can use ordinary bricks (again to match the house), natural stone, timber railway sleepers, or even tree sections. The last three are particularly good choices for rural gardens.

As mentioned earlier, build to any shape desired – square, rectangular, L-shaped or even triangular to fit a corner. As with any container, depth is important to allow the plants to root deeply and to ensure the compost does not dry out rapidly. A good depth is between 45 and 60 cm (18 and 24 in). The walls of beds built with ornamental concrete walling blocks, bricks or stone should be topped with coping stones, either imitation concrete or natural stone. Home-made beds or planters can, if desired, incorporate a seat, simply by setting large paving slabs over part of it.

Beds can be built directly onto an existing paved area, but if you are building a new patio it is wasteful of slabs to lay them where the planters are to be. In this instance the planters can be built on concrete footings. In any event, there must be drainage holes at ground level around the sides of the planter, to allow excess water to escape.

After constructing the beds place a 7.5–10 cm (3–4 in)

In this patio collection the temporary summer bedding plants have a background of permanent evergreen shrubs which help to show to advantage the various colours.

A traditional wooden tub is a good choice of container for a patio in a country garden. This one is planted with 'cool' blue campanulas or bellflowers and pansies.

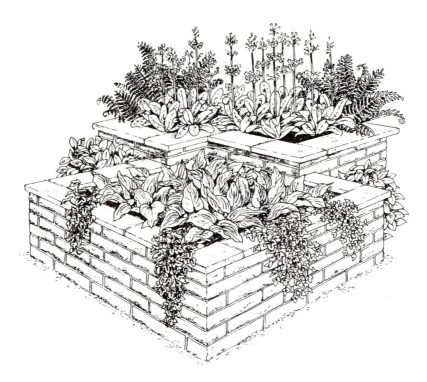

Fig. 11 Raised beds constructed of ornamental concrete walling blocks in stone finish. These beds are suitable for all kinds of plants. Here is a planting scheme for a shady spot: hostas or plantain lilies, trailing ivies, candelabra primulas and ferns. There are many other shade-loving plants that could be included in this scheme.

layer of rubble or pebbles in the bottom to act as a drainage layer, top this with a 2.5 cm (1 in) layer of rough peat or leafmould and then fill with soil or compost. If you need a large volume of soil then, for reasons of economy, buy in a quantity of good-quality topsoil – a light to medium loamy type. Remember that if you want to grow lime-hating plants the soil must be acid: with a ph of below 6.5. As most lime-haters like a humus-rich growing medium, mix plenty of peat or leafmould with the soil before filling the planter.

Planters can, alternatively, be filled with a soil-based potting compost, (but not for lime haters). If you wish to grow alpines then a very gritty, well-drained compost should be used. You can either use light topsoil or proprietary compost, but add to a given volume one-third of coarse horticultural sand or grit. These ingredients should be lime free.

Planting ideas

SHADY AREAS

Raised beds or planters can be placed either in shady or sunny positions and plants chosen accordingly. For instance, if the bed is in shade you could have a delightful collection of peat-garden plants, grown in an acid, peaty compost.

Choose small-growing peat-garden plants, such as dwarf rhododendrons. There is a vast range of these but some of my favourites, which I can particularly recommend, are *Rhododendron impeditum*, a small mound of tiny leaves studded with purplish blue flowers; the prostrate *R. forrestii repens* with scarlet bell-shaped blooms; *R. campylogynum* with waxy bell-shaped flowers in pink or purplish shades; and *R. keiskei* with trusses of lemon-yellow funnel-shaped flowers in early spring.

Good companions for the rhododendrons are the cassiopes, small evergreen shrubs with white bell-like flowers in spring. Well-known species are *C. lycopodioides* and *C. tetragona*. A prostrate, spreading, evergreen shrub which can be allowed to spread over the edge of the planter is *Arctostaphylos uva-ursi* with white urn-shaped blooms in spring, followed by red berries. Small-growing gaultherias should be considered, like *G. trichophylla*, an evergreen with deep pink urn-shaped flowers in spring followed by attractive blue berries.

Lithospermum diffusum is stunning in the intensity of its blue flowers. Try to obtain the variety 'Heavenly Blue'. The flowering period is early summer to mid-autumn. *Phyllodoce aleutica* is a heath-like evergreen with globular, greeny yellow flowers in spring and early summer. Small-growing vacciniums are a good choice, too, like the prostrate, creeping, *V. praestans* with white or reddish bell-shaped flowers in early summer followed by red berries and brilliant autumn leaf colour.

There are two new dwarf pieris which would also be suitable: *Pieris japonica* 'Little Heath', a rounded evergreen shrub with small creamy white variegated leaves and pink-flushed new growth; and *P.j.* 'Little Heath Green' with glossy, bronze-tinted foliage. Surprisingly, these pieris do not produce flowers – they are essentially foliage shrubs.

If you want a more general planting scheme for a shady spot, then try the classical combination of hostas or plantain lilies, with their bold, 'blue', green, yellow or variegated foliage, candelabra primulas, meconopsis or blue poppies, and ferns (Fig. 11). These could be planted around a 'framework' of Japanese maples, varieties of *Acer palmatum*, noted for autumn leaf colour. Winter and spring interest could be provided by Lenten roses (*Helleborus orientalis*) and small bulbs like snowdrops (galanthus) and miniature daffodils (*Narcissus cyclamineus* and *N. bulbocodium*). Spring-flowering miniature cyclamen are recommended too.

SUNNY POSITIONS

In a position which receives plenty of sun why not consider a collection of alpines or rock plants? You could have a miniature rock garden – or perhaps a better description would be a scree bed.

A natural scree is a drift of broken rock at the bottom of a rock face – it does not contain much soil and is therefore very free draining. It makes a home, though, for many choice alpines. Similar conditions are easily created in a raised bed or planter. This feature looks particularly good in a modern setting. Do use a very well-drained compost: 10 parts stone chippings or pea shingle, 1 part loam, 1 part peat and 1 part coarse horticultural sand. Add a little organic slow-release fertilizer such as bonemeal.

A few well-shaped pieces of rock can be bedded into the compost before planting; and after planting the surface of the compost can be covered with a layer of stone chippings (if you cannot obtain these, use pea shingle which is readily available from builders' merchants).

Although many rock plants or alpines will flourish in these conditions, I suggest trying some of the more choice plants, such as *Androsace, Calceolaria, Daphne, Dianthus, Draba, Gentiana, Hebe*, miniature *Iris, Leontopodium* (edelweiss), *Lewisia, Phyteuma, Saxifraga* (of which there is a huge selection), *Sedum, Teucrium* and *Veronica*. Variation in height can be created with dwarf conifers, like junipers and pines.

Also for a modern setting, a bed of heathers and dwarf conifers can be recommended. This would be a truly labour-saving bed and by choosing a good selection of heathers you could have colour all the year round. You will need an acid or lime-free compost or soil, with plenty of peat added.

Dwarf conifers can include the deep gold *Thuja occidentalis* 'Rheingold'; the greyish or bluish green *Juniperus chinensis* 'Pyramidalis'; bright yellow *Chamaecyparis pisifera* 'Filifera Aurea'; bright green

A contemporary container on a modern patio. Ideally some containers should be permanently planted. This one contains a very suitable shrub or small tree – a purple-leaved Japanese maple.

A modern raised bed constructed from ornamental concrete walling blocks, which resemble natural stone. Such beds often feature on or around patios.

Picea glauca 'Albertiana Conica'; and silvery blue *Chamaecyparis pisifera* 'Boulevard'.

Now to the choice of heathers for year-round colour. For winter and spring use any of the varieties (which most appeal to you) of *Erica herbacea* (also known as *E. carnea*), and *Erica* × *darleyensis*. For summer and autumn colour plant varieties of *Calluna vulgaris* (not forgetting some of the superb coloured-foliage varieties for additional winter interest); *Erica cinerea*; *Erica tetralix*; *Daboecia cantabrica*; and *Erica vagans*. Once the heathers have established and formed a dense carpet they will suppress annual weeds. The only attention they need (apart from watering in dry weather) is a light trim after flowering to remove dead flower heads. I would suggest mulching this bed with sphagnum peat to help prevent the surface of the soil from drying out.

RAISED BORDERS

A good way of creating different levels in a small flat garden is to have raised borders. The only ways in which these differ from raised beds or planters is that they are obviously longer (for instance, it may be desired to run the border the length of the plot) and generally they are not so high – a height of 30 cm (12 in) may well be sufficient to create the desired effect. Indeed, if any higher there is a danger the height will not be in proportion to the length. Do not make the borders too narrow – a width of at least 90 cm (3 ft) is recommended.

Construction and filling is the same as for beds and planters, and generally it is not necessary to have a layer of drainage material in the base. But if the garden soil is very poorly drained it should be improved by digging deeply and adding plenty of coarse grit or shingle, before starting to build.

To avoid repetition, suffice it to say that planting ideas for borders are the same as for beds. Of course, there is a much wider range of plants that could be used: there is no reason why climbers should not be planted and trained up the back wall or fence. Shrubs,

provided they are not too large, would be suitable, so long as they are happy with the normal garden soil, for remember that due to the shallow depth of the border they will root down into the soil below. Hardy perennials, bulbs, alpines, bedding plants and hardy annuals are all suitable for raised borders.

DOUBLE WALLS

A double wall for planting is rather like a narrow raised bed. It is often used as a boundary for the front garden, as a feature in front of a porch and for surrounding a patio. The height of the wall will depend on its use: for instance, if it is to form the front boundary it may need to be at least 90 cm (3 ft) high, but slightly lower, if desired, in front of a porch or around a patio. A good width is about 60 cm (2 ft).

Suitable materials for construction include ornamental concrete walling blocks in brick or stone finish to match the house, bricks, or natural walling stone. With the latter you could, if desired, build a dry-stone wall so that trailing plants can be grown in the sides. With a dry-stone wall the joints are not mortared but filled with soil for planting. The stones should be laid at random but interlocked to ensure strength. If desired, plants can be inserted as building proceeds.

Each wall should be built on a substantial strip foundation consisting of well-rammed hardcore topped with concrete. Depth of each about 10 cm (4 in). With long walls it is recommended that cross ties are inserted every 1.2 m (4 ft), extending from one wall to the other, to ensure extra strength. These can consist of iron bars or, in the case of dry-stone walls, long pieces of stone.

The walls should be finished off with coping and then filled with soil or compost, above a layer of drainage material, as described for raised beds (see page 49). Also, do not forget to leave drainage holes along the sides at ground level. Unless sufficient drainage holes are provided, the soil or compost in the wall could become waterlogged, leading to deterioration of the plants.

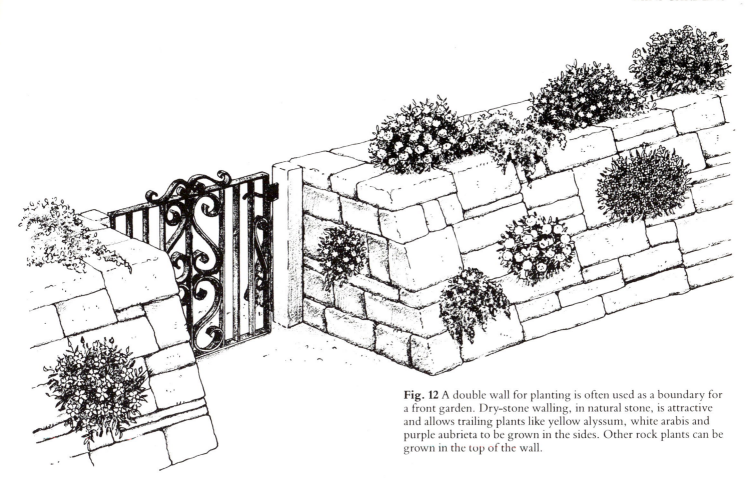

Fig. 12 A double wall for planting is often used as a boundary for a front garden. Dry-stone walling, in natural stone, is attractive and allows trailing plants like yellow alyssum, white arabis and purple aubrieta to be grown in the sides. Other rock plants can be grown in the top of the wall.

Planting ideas

If you want lots of summer colour, perhaps around a patio or in front of a porch, then of course any of the summer bedding plants can be used as described in previous chapters. These can be followed with spring bedding and bulbs. But if you want planting schemes which are a bit out of the ordinary (and indeed labour-saving) then there is a wide range of attractive perm-anent plants that you could choose from.

Rock plants immediately spring to mind. I have already recommended some for raised beds (see page 53), but some of the more popular, showy kinds could be used if you want lots of colour, like the ever-popular yellow *Alyssum saxatile*, blue, purple, red or pink aubrieta, and white arabis (Fig. 12). I know that this particular scheme is very much over-done, but if you want plenty of colour in spring it takes a lot of beating.

Other rock plants you could use include trailing campanulas with blue flowers, like *C. portenschlagiana*, which can be planted in the sides of a dry-stone wall; the rock pinks or dianthus; rock roses or helianthemums

An old stone sink, attractively planted with alpines or rock plants, makes an unusual feature on a patio. Note the raised bed behind, built with dry-stone walling.

These raised beds have been built from imitation railway sleepers and from vertical 'logs' which are supplied in rolls. Both are ideally suited to natural or country gardens.

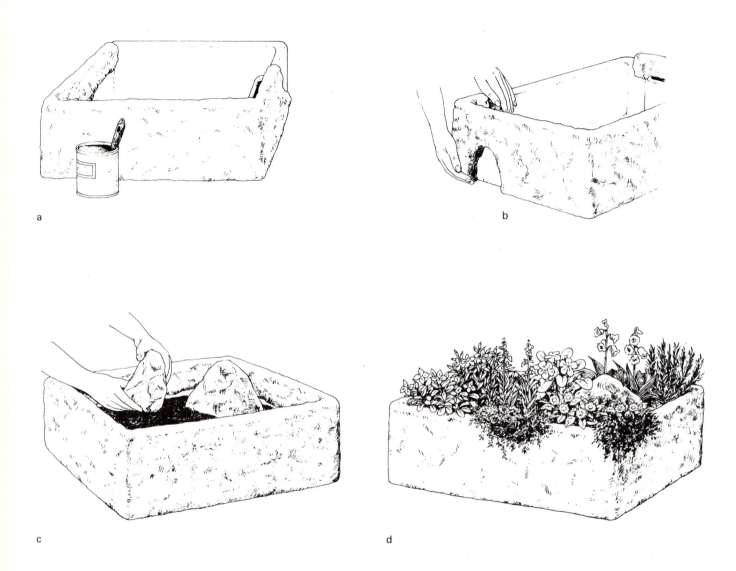

a

b

c

d

Fig. 13 Converting a white-glazed sink so that it resembles stone. First treat with a PVA adhesive (*a*) then, before it completely dries, apply a hypertufa mix (*b*) which consists of peat, cement and sand. Fill with gritty compost and add a few pieces of rock (*c*), then plant with alpines of restrained habit (*d*).

whose single-rose-like flowers come in a wide range of bright colours; the white perennial candytuft or *Iberis sempervirens*; lewisias, which are ideal for planting in the sides of a dry-stone wall, as are the sempervivums or houseleeks; and the creeping thymes, or varieties of *Thymus serpyllum*.

Dwarf bulbs could be planted with the rock plants, such as tulip, crocus and dwarf allium species. These, and the alpines, need plenty of sun.

There are lots of dwarf shrubs which enjoy a sunny spot, including the brooms. Try *Cytisus × beanii* with yellow flowers, and *C. × kewensis*, with sheets of cream blooms, both at their best in late spring. Then there is *Genista lydia* with masses of golden flowers at that time of year. *Daphne arbuscula* is a small evergreen shrub which bears scented pink flowers in early summer. Try some dwarf berberis, too, like the *B. thunbergii* varieties 'Atropurpurea Nana', purple foliage' and 'Kobold' with shiny green leaves. *B. buxifolia* 'Nana' forms an evergreen mound and bears yellow flowers.

Small perennials which would enjoy the dryish conditions of the double wall, and which need full sun, include *Anthemis cupaniana* with attractive greyish foliage and a long succession of white daisy-like flowers in summer and through to autumn. The red valerian, *Centranthus ruber*, can be planted in the sides of a dry-stone wall. It flowers continuously from early to late summer, carrying panicles of deep pink or red flowers, set against glaucous foliage. There is also a white-flowered form, 'Albus'.

The stems of the spurge, *Euphorbia myrsinites*, will trail over the edge of the wall and are clothed with attractive bluish-grey foliage. In the spring acid-yellow flowers are produced. *Oenothera missouriensis* has a similar habit of growth, and throughout summer it bears large saucer-shaped yellow flowers.

The herbaceous potentillas relish sunny, dryish conditions and produce attractive single-rose-like flowers in spring or summer. A particularly attractive species is *Potentilla tabernaemontani* which forms an evergreen mat, studded in spring with yellow flowers.

The stonecrops or sedums will certainly be at home in a wall, and if it is dry-stone can be planted in the sides. Try species like *S. acre*, yellow flowers; *S. album*, white; *S. cauticolum*, red; *S. spathulifolium* and its varieties 'Purpureum' wich purple foliage and the grey-leaved 'Cappa Blanca'; and *S. spurium* with deep pink flowers.

The Californian fuchsia, *Zauschneria californica*, is a somewhat unusual and desirable plant which bears red fuchsia-like flowers in summer and autumn, set against greyish-green foliage.

SINK GARDENS

Sinks make excellent containers for alpines or rock plants, and they form attractive features on both formal and informal patios. One can, in fact, create miniature rock gardens in these containers.

The old shallow stone sinks are worth searching for, but are not easily found these days, for they are scarce collectors' items and demand a high price. The alternative is to convert a white glazed sink so that it resembles stone (Fig. 13). You should be able to pick up one of these quite easily from a scrapyard or local builder for they are frequently discarded with the boom in fitted designer kitchens. Perhaps this is more practical, anyway, for a white glazed sink has a greater depth than the old-fashioned stone versions, so there is less risk of the compost drying out rapidly during warm weather.

A glazed sink is covered with hypertufa, which is a mixture of cement, sand and peat. When this has hardened and has become well weathered it looks like natural tufa rock. Before you apply a hypertufa mix the sink has to be treated with a PVA adhesive, to ensure the hypertufa sticks to the glaze. This adhesive, which is used in the building trade, is available from DIY and hardware stores. Brush it on the outside of the sink and part of the way down on the inside. When it has become tacky (before it completely dries) apply the hypertufa mix.

The hypertufa mix consists of 2 parts sphagnum peat, 1 part sand and 1 part cement – parts by volume.

This raised bed for alpines has been built up with dry-stone walling, which makes an ideal home for various trailing plants. Plants could be set in the sides as building proceeds.

Add sufficient water to make a stiff but pliable mix. Then spread it about 12 mm (½ in) thick all over the treated parts of the sink, firmly pressing it into place with your fingers. Leave a fairly rough texture to resemble natural stone.

The hypertufa will take at least two weeks to harden thoroughly, after which the sink should be filled with a solution of permanganate of potash, and left for at least 24 hours, which will remove any harmful chemicals from the cement. Afterwards wash out the sink thoroughly.

Before filling the sink with compost decide where you want it on the patio – choose the sunniest spot – and then stand it on two rows of bricks, two courses high, to raise it slightly above ground level. The bricks can be bonded with mortar for stability. Place over the bottom of the sink a 2.5 cm (1 in) layer of 'crocks' (broken clay flower pots) to act as drainage. Put a large piece over the drainage hole. Cover the crocks with a thin layer of coarse peat or leafmould. Then fill to within 2.5 cm (1 in) of the top with potting compost. A soil-based type is best for alpines. Add to this one-third extra of coarse horticultural sand or grit to ensure really good drainage. The sand or grit should be free from lime.

Before planting, bed a few pieces of natural rock into the compost to create a mini rock garden. Set rocks to about one-third of their depth into the compost.

Choosing plants

First plant one or two dwarf conifers to give height and contrast in form. The most suitable is the tiny Noah's ark juniper, *Juniperus communis* 'Compressa', with greyish-green prickly foliage.

For the edges of the sink use trailing alpines like *Phlox douglasii*, a mass of lilac flowers in the spring; and the pink, early summer flowering *Aethionema armenum*. The spreading, silvery-leaved *Raoulia hookeri* (also known as *R. australis*), will 'soften' the edges of the sink as it becomes established.

Fill in with more alpines, choosing those of restrained habit so that they do not take over the entire container. Suitable kinds include the thrift, *Armeria caespitosa*, a mound-forming plant studded with pink flowers in the spring; the rose-pink, early summer flowering rock pink, *Dianthus neglectus; Geranium cinereum*, spring flowering, pink blooms; *Gypsophila caucasica*, white flowers in early summer; saxifrages like the white, spring flowering *S.* × *burseriana*; and the cobweb houseleek, *Sempervivum arachnoideum*, whose rosettes of succulent leaves are covered with white webbing, like spiders' webs.

When planting is completed cover the surface of the compost with a thin layer of stone chippings or pea shingle. This will create an attractive appearance and help to ensure good drainage around the plants.

6

DESIGN IDEAS FOR UTILITY PLANTS

Many people with small gardens like to grow some fruits and vegetables and often opt for cultivation in containers on the patio. Certainly many crops are suited to container growing and although essentially utility plants, nevertheless they can, with a little thought, be made to form attractive features in themselves or to combine pleasantly with ornamental plants.

FRUITS

Apples, pears, plums, cherries, peaches, nectarines, grapes and citrus fruits can all be grown in containers as dwarf trained forms.

In my opinion all of these trees are attractive in themselves, especially when in flower and fruit, and therefore no apology should be made for including them on a patio. They can be enhanced by growing them in classical square wooden tubs, painted white (Fig. 14). Diameter and depth should be 45–60 cm (18–24 in). Containers should be filled with a soil-based potting compost, making sure there is a good layer of drainage material in the bottom, such as crocks or broken clay flower pots.

Fruits need a warm, sunny, sheltered spot. Take care with watering to ensure the compost does not dry out, nor becomes excessively wet. Feed once a week in the spring and summer with a high-potash fertilizer. Fruits should be thinned out to ensure the trees do not carry an excess. Fruit trees require regular pruning but

Fig. 14 Dwarf pyramid apple and bush fig in classical square wooden tubs. Both would enhance any patio, as would the grape vine growing in a classical terracotta vase. The grape vine is very amenable to training and for container work is conveniently grown in the form of a standard, as shown here.

as this is quite an involved subject and varies according to the type of fruit and the form in which it is grown, a specialist fruit book should be consulted.

Choosing fruits

Most of the fruits described here are trained as dwarf bush trees or dwarf pyramids and they should be obtained on dwarfing rootstocks to keep them small. With apples and pears you have to grow several varieties to ensure cross-pollination of the flowers, otherwise few if any fruits will be produced. If space is very limited you could grow a 'family' apple or pear tree – which has several varieties grafted onto it.

Apples on dwarfing rootstock M9 or M27 should be bought, and grown as dwarf bush or dwarf pyramid trees. Make sure the varieties cross-pollinate each other. For instance, you could grow together the varieties 'Cox's Orange Pippin', 'Greensleeves', 'Discovery', 'Ashmead's Kernel' and 'Egremont Russet', all good popular varieties.

Pears are grown in the same forms as apples. Again grow at least two varieties to ensure cross pollination: the popular 'Williams' 'Bon Chretien' with 'Conference'; or 'Doyenne du Comice' with 'Beurre Hardy'. All are good well-known varieties.

With cherries buy a self-fertile variety such as 'Stella' which needs no other variety to pollinate it. It should be bought on the dwarfing rootstock 'Colt' and grown as a dwarf pyramid or bush.

Also with plums, buy a self-fertile variety, like the highly popular 'Victoria'. It should be on the dwarf rootstock 'Pixy' and grown as a dwarf pyramid or bush.

Peaches and nectarines are grown as dwarf bush trees. Remember that the flowers, which appear early in the year, have to be pollinated by hand by dabbing the centre of each flower in turn with a soft artist's brush to transfer the pollen.

Citrus fruits, like the sweet orange, *Citrus sinensis*, and the Seville orange, *C. aurantium*, can be grown as dwarf pyramid or bush trees. Remember that these are tender trees and need to be kept in a frost-free greenhouse or conservatory over the winter. Figs must also be overwintered under glass to protect the young developing fruits from frost. Grow figs as bush trees.

The grape vine is very amenable to training and for container work is conveniently grown as standard: that is, a single permanent stem with most new growth being produced at the top. The overall height is about 1.8 m (6 ft). All the shoots which form the 'head' are cut back to within one or two buds of their base each year in early winter.

Strawberries can make an attractive feature on a patio, especially if grown in proprietary Tower Pots on the modern patio; or in strawberry barrels on the cottage patio. The Tower Pot basically consists of a tall cylinder with planting pockets in the sides, while the strawberry barrel is an ordinary timber barrel with 5 cm (2 in) diameter holes drilled in the sides, about 20 cm (8 in) apart, in a staggered formation. The roots of the strawberry plants are inserted through the holes as the barrel is being filled with compost. Finish off with several plants in the top, too.

VEGETABLES

Many vegetables can be grown successfully in growing-bags on the patio, but these containers are far from attractive. They are long – approximately 1.2 m (4 ft) – plastic bags filled with peat-based compost and are generally 'decorated' with the maker's name and other lettering. They are temporary containers, being discarded at the end of the season. Holes are made in the tops of the bags for planting.

Fortunately the bags are easily hidden by surrounding them with pots of colourful summer bedding plants. It pays to grow a few extra plants, individually in 12.5 cm (5 in) pots, specially for hiding growing-bags. Choose bushy or trailing bedding plants for the purpose, which will also hide their own containers, like trailing petunias, verbena, lobelia, alyssum and ivy-leaved pelargoniums. Bedding impatiens can also

Herbs and scented-leaved plants are generally attractive and deserve a place on the patio, ideally planted in dumpy or bowl-shaped containers rather than tall pots.

Citrus fruits, like oranges, look good in white tubs, but bear in mind that they need to be overwintered in a frost-free conservatory or greenhouse.

be recommended as they make very bushy growth.

The majority of vegetables like plenty of sun so bear this in mind when siting growing-bags.

Choice of vegetables

It is sensible, wherever possible, to grow attractive-looking vegetables on the patio – those which contribute colour or some other pleasing feature. Then they will not look too much out of place in this essentially ornamental area.

I consider **beetroots**, with their purple foliage, quite attractive plants and they look good with colourful summer bedding plants. Choose the round-rooted varieties, thinning seedlings to 10 cm (4 in) apart.

Rhubarb chard, a leaf beet, has striking red stems which, together with the leaves, are cooked and eaten. A growing-bag will hold four or five plants.

I also like the ferny foliage of **carrots**, the early varieties of which are well worth growing on the patio. Thin seedlings to 5 cm (2 in) apart each way.

Red chicory, 'Rossa de Verona', has very attractive reddish foliage which is used in salads. A growing-bag will hold about four plants.

For salads, and providing an attractive foil for brightly coloured summer bedding, choose **curled endive**, with green curled foliage. Also with very attractive deeply cut foliage is the non-hearting lettuce 'Salad Bowl'. Here one picks the individual leaves as required. There are lettuces available with reddish foliage. Again, a growing-bag will comfortably hold four or five plants of endive or lettuce.

Tomatoes can be highly decorative, especially if you buy seeds of a mixture of ornamental kinds, which include miniature plum-, currant- and pear-shaped kinds with red and yellow fruits. There are several varieties of cherry tomato and yellow-fruited and striped tomatoes, all of which create colour on the patio. Three to four plants can be accommodated in a growing-bag.

Asparagus peas are highly ornamental with their profusion of red flowers. These are followed by winged pods which are picked and cooked whole, while they are young – absolutely delicious when served with butter. Plants should be spaced about 20 cm (8 in) apart each way.

Climbing French beans are more productive than dwarf varieties and particularly attractive is the aptly named variety 'Purple Podded'. Plants can be spaced 10–15 cm (4–6 in) apart.

Runner beans can also be grown in growing-bags and make a good display when in flower with their red, white or pink flowers, according to variety. Plants can be spaced 10–15 cm (4–6 in) apart.

Climbing vegetables can, of course, be trained to a wall or fence, using netting or a trellis panel as a support. Tall tomatoes can be supported with a proprietary growing-bag crop support, as bamboo canes cannot be used in growing-bags.

There are several other vegetables which are ideally suited to growing-bags, although to be honest they could not, by any stretch of the imagination, be called decorative. Nevertheless you may wish to grow them: they include radishes, spring or salad onions, outdoor cucumbers, dwarf early peas and dwarf French beans.

HERBS

Most herbs are fairly or very attractive and therefore deserve a place on the patio, ideally near the kitchen door where they can be easily picked when preparing meals.

Herbs deserve to be grown in attractive containers and I would particularly recommend dumpy or bowl-shaped terracotta pots, either decorated or plain (Fig. 15). In any event the containers should not be too tall as most herbs are quite short plants. Terracotta is particularly suitable for herbs as it is a porous material and does not result in the compost remaining wet for long periods, which is anathema to herbs, which like very well drained and well-aerated compost.

Terracotta troughs would also make good containers for herbs and so, too, would window-boxes, perhaps in the same material, or constructed of wood.

Fig. 15 Herbs deserve to be grown in attractive containers, such as these classical-style bowl-shaped pots, and trough, in terracotta. Seen here are a clipped bay (*a*), sage (*b*), thyme (*c*), chives (*d*) and mint (*e*). An attractive group, ideal for placing conveniently near the kitchen door.

Parsley pots – those terracotta pots with holes in the sides – can certainly be used for parsley, but they are probably not suitable for many other types of herbs. In fact, I don't use them for herbs at all, much preferring to grow summer bedding plants in them.

Herbs must be grown in the warmest, sunniest spot available on the patio (with the exception of mint which will thrive in shade or semi-shade, although it will not object to sun).

I have already mentioned that herbs like well-drained conditions and this means crocking the pots well and then filling them with a soil-based compost. I generally like to add some extra coarse lime-free, horticultural sand or grit to this, particularly if a bit on the heavy side, to keep it open and well drained and aerated.

A collection of herbs is an idea for a patio planter – they would certainly help to provide a Mediterranean atmosphere.

Choice of herbs

There is a wide range of herbs available for culinary use but you may find the following most useful.

Mint, of course, is virtually essential if you want mint sauce for lamb and wish to flavour new potatoes. It grows well in shade, needs plenty of moisture and should be planted about 15 cm (6 in) apart each way. It is best confined to a pot as it is a vigorous grower: it could get out of hand in a planter.

Parsley is also a much-used herb and is raised annually in spring from seeds which, it is worth noting, are very slow to germinate. Thin out seedlings to 15 cm (6 in) apart each way.

The leaves of **chives** are used to impart onion flavourings to dishes. Space small clumps about 15 cm apart each way. Lift and divide them every couple of years or so.

Sage can be raised from seeds or young plants bought in spring. The leaves are used for flavouring meats. If you want more than one plant, set the plants 30 cm (12 in) apart each way.

Thyme, which is used for flavouring meats and poultry, can also be raised from seeds, sown in spring, or young plants can be bought, setting them 20 cm (8 in) apart each way.

Rosemary makes quite a large shrub eventually and therefore only one plant is usually needed. The leaves are often used in meat casseroles, and are particularly good for flavouring lamb.

The sweet bay is a large evergreen shrub and makes

an attractive clipped specimen in a wooden tub. The leaves are used in all kinds of cooking. It is not too hardy and in cold areas would be better overwintered in a frost-free greenhouse or conservatory.

Fennel is a very attractive perennial plant with ferny foliage. It grows up to 1.8 m (6 ft) in height and is therefore better suited to the back of a planter or raised bed.

The leaves are used mainly for flavouring fish. Generally a single plant is sufficient. It will thrive in sun or slight shade and prefers moist soil.

Oregano or wild marjoram is a perennial with pinkish flowers in summer. The leaves are used in all kinds of dishes – especially Italian and Provencal. Plant about 20 cm (8 in) apart each way.

7

PREPARATIONS AND CARE

To ensure that plants establish and grow well containers should be properly prepared and a suitable compost used to fill them. Compost must be changed regularly for both temporary and permanent plants as it gradually deteriorates. Permanent plants may, of course, outgrow their containers and need moving on to a larger size. As with plants in beds and borders, regular feeding is needed in the growing season. And regular watering will be needed – perhaps once or twice a day in warm weather. One should not simply forget plants in the winter; at this time they are at their most vulnerable and they could suffer or die if the compost remains frozen solid for long periods. All of these aspects of container preparation and care are discussed in this chapter. As you can see, container growing is not exactly labour-saving, but nevertheless can be very rewarding.

POSITIONING AND SITING

From the design point of view positioning and siting of containers has been covered in detail in previous chapters, but some thought should also be given to the practical aspects of placing containers.

Try to avoid siting containers in wind tunnels, as may occur in the gaps between houses. Wind rushes through these gaps and can cause damage to plants, such as foliage scorch; and large leaves can be torn. Also, wind contributes to rapid drying out of compost. At all costs avoid placing hanging baskets in windy places – for the obvious reason that they will be rocked around by the wind. If this happens, the plants are likely to be damaged.

I have already covered the subject of sun and shade and recommended many plants for both situations. Just a reminder here, then, to choose plants accordingly – plants which like the sun will not grow or flower well in shady conditions and often produce very weak growth. Many shade-loving plants can suffer scorched foliage if subjected to too much sun.

If drips from window boxes are liable to be a problem (for example, with boxes on the balconies of flats and apartments) then place drip trays under them to catch surplus water. Do make sure that containers are not in very close contact with the ground for this can impede the drainage of surplus water and result in saturated compost, which can cause roots of plants to rot. And make sure that a seal of soil does not build up around the base of containers, which again effectively prevents drainage of water. It's a good idea to very slightly raise containers above the ground to allow drainage, only a fraction of an inch – say about 6 mm (¼ in) – so that it is barely noticeable. This can be achieved with pieces of wooden lath, but make sure they do not cover drainage holes nor protrude beyond the container.

DRAINAGE MATERIALS

All containers for plants such as tubs, urns, pots and window boxes must have drainage holes in the base to allow excess water to escape. Before filling with compost and planting, these drainage holes must be covered with a layer of drainage material. Traditionally 'crocks' or broken clay flower pots are used. Large pieces are placed over the holes and then a layer of smaller pieces placed over these. Total depth should be at least 2.5 cm (1 in).

There is one pot manufacturer in Britain who actually supplies purpose-made crocks – made from fired ceramic material. Alternatives to crocks are large shingle and horticultural aggregates.

The drainage layer must be covered with a thin layer of rough organic material to prevent compost from washing down and blocking it. Suitable materials are rough leafmould or peat, or pulverized bark.

Composts

On no account fill containers such as tubs, urns, pots, window boxes and hanging baskets with ordinary garden soil as it may not be sufficiently well drained and aerated. Far better to use a proprietary or home-made potting compost, which will also contain a good balance of fertilizers. Certainly large planters, raised beds, double walls, etc, can be filled with good-quality topsoil, ideally a light to medium loamy type, as a large volume of potting compost can be quite expensive to buy. I have already given some recommendations of composts for various types of plants but let us go into the subject in a bit more detail.

There are two basic types of potting compost that we can use in containers – the type containing loam (or soil) and the soilless or all-peat composts. Soilless composts are very light in weight and ideal for hanging baskets and window boxes, although they can be used in other types of container, too. Ericaceous plants like rhododendrons and heathers, and camellias,

flourish in them, although bear in mind that they may not adequately support large heavy plants. For lime-hating plants you should, of course, use an acid or lime-free compost (generally sold as ericaceous compost).

You should also bear in mind that soilless composts must not be firmed too much, plant foods are quickly leached out so more regular feeding will be needed; they should not be allowed to dry out as it is very difficult to wet them again; and that they are inclined to hold more water than soil-based composts, so if you are very heavy-handed with the watering can the compost may become too wet.

The heavier soil-based composts are ideal for large heavy plants, especially permanent kinds. Again use a lime-free compost for lime-hating plants. This type of compost drains well, contains a good supply of air for the plants' roots and is able to hold on to its fertilizers for much longer than soilless composts. If a soil-based compost dries out it is not too difficult to moisten again, and there is little risk of saturating the compost with water.

It generally works out cheaper to mix your own composts and this is especially worth while if you want a large volume. Here are some standard formulae:

SOIL-BASED POTTING COMPOST

7 parts loam
3 parts peat
2 parts sand
Parts by volume and all mixed together very thoroughly.

To every bushel (8 gallons or 36 litres) of this mix add 113 g (4 oz) of potting base fertilizer and 21 g (¾ oz) ground limestone or chalk.

Most plants, however, prefer a slightly richer compost, so add to each bushel 226 g (8 oz) of potting base fertilizer and 42 g (1½ oz) ground limestone or chalk.

An even richer compost, ideal for most large permanent plants like shrubs, trees and fruits, can be made by adding to each bushel 340 g (12 oz) of potting base fertilizer and 63 g (2¼ oz) ground limestone or chalk.

You can buy loam in bags from garden centres. Try to obtain a light or medium loam, which should have been partially sterilized by the producer, and ideally slightly acid, with a pH of 6–6.5. For lime-hating plants it must be more acid than this – pH 5–5.5.

The ideal peat is granulated sphagnum-moss peat which is bought in bags or bales from garden centres. The sand should be a horticultural type, free from lime and quite coarse.

If the compost is for lime-hating plants omit the ground limestone or chalk from the mix.

SOILLESS POTTING COMPOST

3 parts peat

1 part sand (or alternatively, use vermiculite or perlite)

Add to this mix a proprietary potting-base fertilizer (acid for lime-haters), the amount being as indicated by the maker.

This mix is suitable for lime-hating plants; or it can be modified if desired: for example, you could incorporate 1 part of acid loam and 1 part of leafmould, and omit the base fertilizer, but this modification is optional.

PLANTING TECHNIQUES

Before planting, wet the rootball of the plant if it is dry, as afterwards it is difficult if not impossible to wet it and the plant may not establish. The easiest way to wet a dry rootball is to stand the plant, complete with its nursery container, in a bucket of water almost up to the rim of the container, for an hour or so.

To plant a single plant in a tub, pot, etc, first place a layer of compost in the bottom, over the drainage material. This must be of sufficient depth that when planting is complete the top of the rootball is 12 mm (½ in) below the level of the new compost and there is a 12–25 mm (½–1 in) watering space (according to size of container) at the top. This layer of compost should be firmed moderately if soil-based, or lightly if soil-less.

Carefully remove the plant from its nursery container, avoiding root disturbance. If in a pot the easiest way to remove it is to invert the pot and tap the rim on a solid object so that the rootball is loosened and slides out. If the plant is in a flexible polythene bag simply slit this down one side and underneath and peel it off. Place the plant in the centre of the tub, etc, and trickle compost all round it, at the same time firming moderately if soil-based and lightly if soilless. Firm with your fingers.

If you are planting several plants in containers, such as spring or summer bedding plants, then it is easiest to fill the container with compost first and then make a planting hole for each, say with a trowel.

Bedding plants are often planted bare-root – in other words, lifted from trays or boxes, with very little soil around the roots. Do ensure the roots do not dry out before planting, so only lift a few plants at a time. Holes for bare-root plants must be sufficiently deep to allow the roots to dangle straight down to their full extent – roots crammed into shallow holes can result in the plants failing to grow well. Planting depth should be the same – in other words, do not plant more deeply nor more shallowly.

After planting, water the plants heavily as this helps to settle the compost around them.

Before planting wire hanging baskets first line them inside with sphagnum moss, with one of the proprietary basket liners or with a piece of polythene with drainage holes in it. Black polythene is least conspicuous. You can then insert plants through the wires in the sides of the basket to provide a ball of colour. Plants should be inserted as the basket is being filled with compost. Carefully push the roots through and cover them with compost. Do not forget to leave a good watering space at the top – about 2.5 cm (1 in). To make a hanging basket more stable when planting stand it on a flower pot of suitable size.

When planting growing-bags make holes in the top as directed by the makers. Do not make drainage holes in the bottom (you will have to be careful with watering to avoid having saturated compost). It is essential to stand growing-bags on a completely level surface.

CHANGING COMPOSTS

When growing plants in tubs, urns, pots and similar containers, and in window boxes and hanging baskets, you should periodically give them a fresh supply of compost, for potting composts deteriorate eventually, with drainage and aeration becoming poor and plant foods depleted.

Potting on

Single plants are best started off in small containers and potted-on (or moved on) to containers two sizes larger before they become pot-bound (container packed with roots). This is better than putting a small plant in a very big container as then it will have a large volume of compost around its roots which may then remain very wet with possibility of root-rot. Of course, if you are starting off with a large plant then it would be more practical to give it a large final-size container to start with.

The best time of year for potting-on is in early spring and the technique is as described under Planting Techniques for single plants in containers, on page 73.

Re-potting

Single permanent plants in large final tubs, pots, etc, should ideally be re-potted every other year to give them a fresh supply of compost. Again early spring is the best time.

It will take two people to handle a large plant. Firstly, the container should be placed on its side. Then one person taps the rim of the container with a block of wood. At the same time the second person gently and steadily pulls the plant. Hopefully the rootball should slide out. If it doesn't insert a long thin blade all round the inside, between container wall and rootball. Then try again.

Reduce the soilball in size by carefully teasing away about 5 cm (2 in) of compost from the sides, bottom and top. If necessary roots can be pruned back by this amount.

Then scrub out the container with water to remove all traces of compost and allow it to dry thoroughly. In the meantime keep the rootball of the plant covered with wet sacking to prevent drying out.

Finally replace the plant in its container, using new compost, which must be worked right down to the bottom. There should be no air spaces.

In the years between re-potting, or if you find you are unable to re-pot, topdressing can be carried out in spring. Remove about 2.5 cm (1 in) of old compost from the top and replace with the same depth of new compost.

Other techniques

If containers are used only for temporary plants like spring and summer bedding it is advisable to completely change the compost every two years or so – certainly before it starts to deteriorate.

With hanging baskets which are used for temporary plants it is usual to discard the compost at the end of each season.

Eventually hanging baskets and window boxes which contain collections of small permanent plants will become overgrown and that is the time for complete replacement – of compost and plants. Plants need not necessarily be discarded: they could be planted in the garden.

The same advice applies to sink gardens. Remember that small perennials and alpines can often be split or divided into smaller portions, so you do not necessarily have to buy new plants. Double walls may need rejuvenating every so often when they become overcrowded.

Raised beds and borders and large planters can be left for several years, just as beds in the garden. It should not be necessary to disturb shrubs, trees, roses, climbers, etc, but every three of four years it is a good idea to lift and divide any perennials and groups of bulbs. With the former this is best done in early spring; while bulbs are lifted, separated and replanted when they are dormant.

FEEDING

Once plants are established and well rooted into the compost a feeding programme can commence. For instance, with subjects planted in spring you can start feeding in summer. With autumn-planted subjects feeding can commence in the following spring.

Only apply feeds during the growing seasons – that is, spring, summer and early autumn. On average, plants in containers can be fed every two weeks, but if pot-bound weekly feeding would be better.

Use a compound general-purpose or flower-garden fertilizer containing the major plant foods nitrogen, phosphorus and potash. Liquid feeding is preferable for container-grown plants and certainly the most convenient means of applying foods. A fertilizer high in potash (for example, 10 per cent nitrogen, 10 per cent phosphorus and 27 per cent potash) is useful for flowering and fruiting plants.

Granular general-purpose or flower-garden fertilizer is best for raised beds, borders and large planters, applying an annual topdressing in spring and lightly forking it into the soil surface.

WATERING

Do not wait until the compost becomes bone-dry before watering as plants can suffer from this: flower buds and foliage can drop. Various plants, like camellias, rhododendrons, fuchsias and conifers soon react to dry compost by dropping leaves and/or flower buds. So regularly inspect containers, testing the compost surface for moisture content with your fingers. If it is drying out on the surface then apply water. Alternatively you could test the state of the compost with a soil-moisture meter.

Apply enough water so that it actually drains out of the bottom of the container; then you know that the compost has been moistened right the way through. Do not apply any more water until the surface is starting to dry out again (too much water can be harmful).

In warm weather containers should be checked once or twice a day for water requirements, and indeed may need watering once or twice, especially hanging baskets. Do check containers in winter, too, for although they dry out slowly the compost can still become dry.

If you have many containers to water you may find a watering lance useful, attached to the end of a hosepipe. With one of these it is an easy matter to water hanging baskets.

If you are away a lot in the spring and summer you may need to consider an automatic watering system. Ideal for containers is the drip system with many thin tubes 'sprouting' from a main hose. The thin tubes are positioned over the compost in the containers. Such a system can be fed either from an elevated water reservoir or from the mains water supply via a header tank with ballcock valve.

If you grow lime-hating plants beware of 'hard' or limy tap water. Occasional use of this does no harm but regular use can result in chlorosis of the leaves (the foliage turns yellow). Instead, try to collect and use rainwater.

WINTER PROTECTION

Many modern containers are frost-proof (that is, they are not damaged by frost), including many terracotta types. However it is the plants that we have to worry about in winter, for they can be severely damaged or killed if the compost remains frozen solid for a pro-longed period.

To help reduce this problem wrap containers thickly with straw, held in place with wire netting. Alternatively put plants in a cool but frost-free greenhouse or conservatory for the winter, particularly those which are liable to be damaged like camellias, African lilies (agapanthus) and hardy fuchsias.

In cold parts of the country which are subjected to hard winters it certainly pays to overwinter plants under glass – certainly most evergreens will not withstand compost which is frozen solid over a long period. I have found that spring bedding plants and bulbs suffer too, or may be killed, if left out all winter in cold areas.

In cold parts of the country it pays to grow as many very hardy plants as possible if you do not relish taking all your containers under glass, and to insulate the containers as described above. Tough evergreen plants include many of the dwarf junipers, the yew *Taxus canadensis*, dwarf varieties of *Thuja occidentalis*, dwarf varieties of *Prunus laurocerasus*, and varieties of ivy, *Hedera helix*.

In very hot areas the compost in containers can heat up excessively and so wherever possible the containers should be shaded in some way, perhaps with plenty of foliage trailing over them.

INDEX

Abutilon striatum 'Thompsonii', 36
Acanthus spinosus, 45
Acer palmatum, 44, 53
Aethionema armenum, 63
Agapanthus 'Headborne Hybrids', 45
Agave americana 'Marginata', 36, 37
Ageratum, 28, 40
Alchemilla mollis, 48
Alpines *see* Rock plants
Alyssum saxatile, 57
Amaranthus, 37
Annuals for foliage, 36–37
Anthemis cupaniana, 61
Apple, 65
Arabis, 57
Aralia elata, 41
Arctostaphyllos uva-ursi, 51
Armeria caespitosa, 63
Arum lily, 20
Asparagus densiflorus
    'Sprengeri', 25
Asparagus pea, 68
Aucuba japonica 'Variegata', 25
Azalea, dwarf, 44
    Kurume hybrids, 25

Background plants, 16
Balcony containers, 32
Barrel containers, 20
Bay, 16, 41
    sweet, 69–70
Bedding plants, 73
    for patios, 37–40
    for window boxes, 25–28
Beetroot, 68
Begonia, pendulous, 29
    semperflorens, 25, 37
    tuberous, 25
Bellis perennis, 25, 29
Berberis thunbergii, 61
    buxifolia 'Nana', 61

Bergenia, 48
Beschorneria yuccoides, 45
Black-eyed susan, 29
Bulbs, dwarf, 45, 61
    for patio, 40
    for window boxes, 25
Busy lizzie, 37
Buxus sempervirens, 20, 41

Cabbage tree, 25, 36
Calceolaria rugosa, 25, 28
    'Sunshine', 29
Calendula officinalis, 40
Calluna vulgaris, 56
Camellia, 16, 44
Campanula isophylla, 25
    persicifolia, 48
    portenschlagiana, 57
Candytuft, perennial, 61
Canna × *generalis*, 36
Carnations, 40
Cassiope, 53
Castor-oil plant, 36
Centranthus ruber, 61
Century plant, 36, 37
Chamaecyparis lawsoniana
    'Ellwoodii', 24, 44
    'Ellwood's Gold', 25, 44
    pisifera, 44
    'Boulevard', 56
    'Filifera Aurea', 53
Cherry, 65
Chicory, red, 68
Chionodoxa, 25
Chives, 69
Chlorophytum comosum
    'Variegatum', 25
Choisya ternata, 48
Chrysanthemum, charm, 28, 29, 37
    frutescens, 28
Citrus fruits, 36, 65

Classical style containers, 16
Clay bell pots, 17
Clematis, 44
Climbers for patios, 44, 48
Coleus, 28, 36
Colour in patio containers, 37
    in window boxes, 24
Composts, 72–73
    changing, 74–75
Conifers, 44
Containers, as focal points, 12–16
    composts for, 72–73
    drainage, 71
    for courtyards and patios, 17–20
    for framing, 20
    for house decoration, 21–32
    for patios, 33–48
    moving, 33
    planting up, 73–74
    siting, 71
    sizes, 40–41, 33
    styles, 8
    uses, 8–9
Cordyline australis, 25, 36
Cotinus coggygria, 16
Cotoneaster 'Hybridus Pendulus', 48
Cotton lavender, 25
Courtyard containers, 17–20
Crataegus oxyacantha 'Paul's
    'Scarlet', 48
Creeping jenny, 24, 29
Crocus chrysanthus, 25
Cytisus × *beanii*, 61
    × *kewensis*, 61

Daboecia cantabrica, 56
Daffodils, dwarf, 25, 53
Dahlia, dwarf bedding, 37
Daisy, Livingstone, 37
Daphne arbuscula, 61
    odora 'Aureomarginata', 48

Day lily, 45
Delphinium hybrids, 48
Dianthus chinensis, 28
  neglectus, 63
  rockery, 57
Drainage, 72
Drip trays, 71

Echeveria glauca, 36
Elaeagnus pungens 'Maculata', 41
Endive, curled, 68
Erica cinerea, 56
  × *darleyensis*, 56
  herbacea, 25, 29, 44, 56
  tetralix, 56
  vagans, 56
Eryngium agavifolium, 45
  bromeliifolium, 45
Euonymus fortunei 'Emerald and
    Gold', 25, 41
  japonicus 'Aureopictus', 41
Eucalyptus globulus, 36
Euphorbia myrsinites, 61
  wulfenii, 45

Fatsia japonica, 16, 17, 41
Feeding, 75
Fennel, 70
Fig, 65
Focal points, 12–16
Foliage plants, 36–37
French bean, 68
Fruits in containers, 64–65
Fuchsia, 25, 37, 48
  Californian, 61

Gardener's garters, 16
Gaultheria trichophylla, 53
Gazania, 37
Genista lydia, 61
Geranium cinereum, 63
Glechoma hederacea 'Variegata', 25

Grape vine, 44, 65
Grasses, 45
Ground ivy, variegated, 25
Growing bags, 9, 73
Gypsophila caucasica, 63

Hanging baskets, 28–29, 73, 74
Hebe × *franciscana*, 48
  pinguifolia 'Pagei', 25
  rakaiensis, 48
Hedera canariensis 'Gloire de
    Marengo', 44
  colchica 'Dentata Variegata', 44
  helix, 25, 29, 41, 44
Helianthemum, 57
Helichrysum petiolatum, 28, 37
Helleborus orientalis, 45, 53
Hemerocallis, 45
Herbs, 68–70
Holly, 41
Honeysuckle, 48
Hosta, 17, 45, 53
Houseleek, cobweb, 63
Hydrangea macrophylla, 45, 48
Hypertufa, 61–63

Iberis sempervirens, 61
Ilex aquifolium 'Ferox Argentea', 41
  crenata 'Golden Gem', 41
Impatiens, 25, 37
Indian shot, 36
Ivy, 25, 29, 41, 44

Jasminum nudiflorum, 48
  officinale, 48
Juniperus chinensis
    'Pyramidalis', 53
  communis 'Compressa', 24, 63
  × *media* 'Blaauw', 44
  'Mint Julep', 44

Kniphofia caulescens, 45

Lady's mantle, 48
Laurel, 16
  dwarf, 44
  spotted, 25
Laurus nobilis, 16, 41
Laurustinus, 16
Lavandula angustifolia
    'Munstead', 25
Lead containers, 16
Lenten rose, 45, 53
Lettuce, 68
Lewisia, 61
Lithospermum diffusum, 53
Lobelia, 40
Lonicera periclymenum 'Belgica', 48
Lupin hybrids, 48
Lysimachia nummularia, 24, 29

Malus floribunda, 44
Marble containers, 17
Marigold, African dwarf, 28
  pot, 40
Meconopsis, 53
Mesembryanthemum criniflorum, 37
Mexican orange blossom, 48
Mimulus, 37
Mint, 69
Muscari, 25

Narcissus, miniature, 53
Nasturtium, 40
  'Alaska', 29
Nectarine, 65
Nemesia strumosa, 40
Nerium oleander, 17, 20, 36
New Zealand flax, 45
Nicotiana, 40

Oenothera missouriensis, 61
Oleander, 17, 36
Oregano, 70
Oriental style containers, 16

Pansy, winter-flowering, 25, 29, 40
Parsley, 69
Parthenocissus tricuspidata, 44
Patio containers, 17–20, 33–48
Peach, 65
Pear, 65
Pelargonium, 28
  ivy-leaved, 29, 40
  zonal, 37
Perennials, hardy, 45, 48
Periwinkle, lesser, 24, 29
Pernettya mucronata 'Bell's
      Seedling', 25
Petunia, 37, 40
  'Resisto', 29
Phalaris arundinacea 'Picta', 16
Phlox douglasii, 63
Phormium, 45
Phyllodoce aleutica, 53
Picea glauca 'Albertiana Conica', 56
Pieris formosa forrestii, 41
  japonica, dwarf, 53
Plantain lily, 17
Pinks, 40, 57, 63
Planters, 49–56, 75
Plum, 65
Potentilla tabernaemontani, 61
Potting-on, 74
Primrose, 25, 29
Primula, candelabra, 53
Prunus 'Amanogawa', 44
  laurocerasus, 16
    'Otto Luyken', 44
Pyrus salicifolia 'Pendula', 44

Raised beds and borders, 49–56, 75

Raoulia hookeri, 63
Re-potting, 74
Rhododendron, 44, 53
Rhubarb chard, 68
Ricinus communis, 36
Robinia pseudoacacia 'Frisia', 44
Rock plants, 53–56
  for double walls, 57
  for sink gardens, 63
Rock rose, 57
Rodgersia pinnata 'Superba', 45
Rosemary, 16, 69
Roses, 44–45
  for patio, 48
  miniature, 24
Rosmarinus officinalis, 16
Runner bean, 68

Sage, 69
Salix caprea 'Pendula', 44
Santolina chamaecyparissus, 44
Saxifraga × *burseriana*, 63
Scilla, 25
Sedum, 61
Sempervivum, 61, 63
Senecio cineraria, 37
Shade-loving plants, 25, 29, 52–53, 71
Shrubs, 36, 45–48
Sink gardens, 61–63, 74
Skimmia reevesiana, 24, 44
Smoke bush, 16
Snowdrops, 25
Sorbus 'Joseph Rock', 44
Steps, containers for, 20
Strawberry, 65
Sweet pea, dwarf, 28, 29, 40

Taxus baccata, 16, 48
Terracotta pots, 16
Thuja occidentalis 'Rheingold', 53
Thunbergia alata, 29
Thyme, 69
Thymus serpyllum, 61
Tomato, 68
Tower Pots, 9, 65
Trachycarpus fortunei, 17, 44
Trailing plants, 21–24
Trees, 48

Vaccinium praestans, 53
Vegetables, 65–68
Verbena, 40
Viburnum davidii, 44
  tinus, 16
Vinca minor, 24, 29
Vine, 44, 65
Virginia creeper, 44
Vitis 'Brant', 44

Wall pots, 29–32
Walls, double, 56–61
Watering, 75
Window boxes, 21–28, 71, 74
Winter protection, 75–76
Wood barrels, 20
  window boxes, 21

Yew, 16
Yucca, 44

Zantedeschia aethiopica, 20
Zauschneria californica, 61

APPENDIX

A SELECTION OF SUPPLIERS/MANUFACTURERS OF GARDEN CONTAINERS

T. Crowther and Son Ltd,
282 North End Road,
Fulham, London, SW6.

Haddonstone Ltd,
The Forge House,
East Haddon,
Northampton, NN6 8DB.

A. Harris and Sons,
Farnham Pottery,
Pottery Lane,
Wrecclesham,
Farnham,
Surrey, GU10 4QJ.

Olive Tree Trading Company Ltd,
Twickenham Trading Estate,
Rugby Road,
Twickenham,
Middlesex, TW1 1DG.

Red Bank Manufacturing Company Ltd,
Measham,
Burton-on-Trent,
Staffordshire, DE12 7EL.

Whichford Potteries,
Whichford,
Shipston-on-Stour,
Warwickshire, CV36 5PG.